ALL I NEED TO KNOW I LEARNED FROM THE GOLDEN GIRLS

THE UPDATED BIGGER, BETTER, BLANCHIER EDITION

T. ANN PRYOR

STAYING GOLDEN

"Look, you didn't ask me for my opinion, but I'm old, so I'm giving it anyway." -Sophia

Lately I find myself wondering what those four sassy old broads in Florida would have made of today's political, moral, and cultural climates. I'm not really sure if we're that far removed from life in the 1980s, yet it feels as though everything is forever changed and somehow still the same.

Perhaps it's that mass media, technology, and other innovations bombard us with global imagery, illustrating that the world is deteriorating at an alarming rate.

Each day it is a new threat of some kind to our way of life. Here, in the United States, we are told that our new enemies are nameless, faceless bogeymen whose ideologies are decidedly anti-American. There is a daily barrage from various media outlets warning us that we are no longer safe. Not that we ever were, but, one could argue that it may have felt that way. My mother, for one, makes that argument all the time and stubbornly stands by her opinion that things were safer and simpler when she was a kid.

Picture it: upstate New York, the 1950s. On a cold and snowy day, a young girl is trudging uphill through the freezing snow lugging a case that contains her most treasured possession… her bowling ball. I'm sure all of our parents have that, "You think your life is hard…" story that is bursting with some kind of drudgery that they endured so we could be grateful that life has improved (all due to their sacrifices). Yeah, my mom's version had a bowling ball. Oh, and she lived in a cozy hamlet replete with ice storms so severe that the entire berg (as in iceberg I'm sure) would (and I think still does) shut down for a week.

Mom laments all the time, wishing she could be back there in her teeny, tiny, frigid, hazardous-to-your-health-because-a-falling-icicle-could-kill-you-hometown. When she does this, I usually stare at her with a glassy eyed look, thinking to myself, "Why? Why would you want to endure that torture?"

But back to the kinder, gentler, America. My mother regularly points to the unsubstantiated fact that sixty odd years ago, "Nobody" locked their doors at night. Apparently children ran rampant through neighborhoods audaciously accepting candy from strangers, and women could walk through town without danger of molestation, ogling, or any other harassment.

To be fair, when put on the spot as to the notion of there being *no crime* while she was growing up, my mom does admit that there were a scandalous three-person homicide when she was in high school. She seems to remember it had to do with a drug deal gone south, and maybe a gang. Also, one of her relatives may have been a suspect. But I digress…

So, if the 1950s were as innocent and childlike as my mother describes then the 1980s must have seemed like a bloodbath in comparison. In a report by Radford College there were more serial killers on the prowl in the U.S. during the 1980s than any of the decades before it or since. Seriously, it's a miracle we made it out alive. The "Me, Me, Me Decade" was chock-a-block full of killers. Not to mention, there a Cold War was raging, terrorists hijacking planes, the Challenger exploded, Reagan was shot, John Lennon was assassinated, Madonna writhed on stage at the inaugural MTV Video Awards (its possible she's still doing that), it was a mess. We had foreign debts, homeless vets, AIDS, Crack, Bernie Goetz... and while we didn't start the fire (Billy Joel did) we were having a hell of time trying to put it out.

Yet, for all of its violence, the 1980s was also an era of progression and movement. For women, the labors of those who had worked tirelessly for equal rights in the 60s and 70s were starting to bear fruit. Films such as *Working Girl* and *Baby Boom* showed us women in the workforce as more than secretaries or typists. In the case of the latter the protagonist was a woman who was determined to not be defined by motherhood (well, she did initially anyway).

Meanwhile, over on television, Designing Women and Murphy Brown featured female characters who were intelligent and opinionated while at the same time forceful, fearless, and not willing to suffer fools lightly. More importantly, however, they were flawed. The typical female stereotype on television had most often been women like Carol Brady, June Cleaver, and Miriam Cunningham. They were the embodiment of the ideal middle-class white woman who was happy to stay at home and raise her children, feed her family, and do the housework. These boilerplate "moms" were great in that this particular archetype frequently makes us, the viewer, feel good. Yet, they really were not and are not representative of real women.

Real women are flawed, trust me, I know firsthand. Modern television does a much better job of illustrating this point and there is a plethora of shows that strive to bring us different types of female characters who are presented in an assortment of situations. Yet, in the 1980s, complex, personality rich, flawed women were not yet readily available. We had had Maude, Florida Evans, Louise Jefferson, Lucy Ricardo, and Mary Richards who were sassier, more opinionated, and more substantial embodiments of women. However, they were still not quite the neurotic messes most of us feel like.

Then, in 1985 a change came, or rather a show came that

presented to the audience, not one, but four, very real, struggling women collectively known as The Golden Girls. They were funny, they were flawed, and they were fabulous.

What made the Golden Girl's, or the GG's, as my husband calls them, so relatable was that they were similar to the women in our daily lives. What made them awesome was that they were our grandmother's age. The show's creators didn't just bring to life four sassy women making it work from day to day. Instead, they brought to life four sassy women who were also much closer to the grave than the cradle which is inherently the brilliance of the show.

By creating characters who were sixty and not twenty, it made their shenanigans and issues frame-able in a manner that said, "Oh. Well, if it's okay for my grandma to like or do that, then maybe it's okay for me too." This concept was unheard of on television prior to the show, and since it went off the air in 1992 there have been any number of attempts to recapture the magic that these four characters made together. And characters they were…

Blanche wantonly hustled after men and was neither ashamed nor abashed by her sexual conduct. She was like a one woman frat house, intent on getting laid above all else. Dorothy was smart and reveled in that fact often to her own chagrin. Rose was naive, but she also saved the day on many an occasion and battled real life problems like age discrimination. Sophia was cantankerous, mouthy, and everything I want to be as an octogenarian. She didn't let anyone get in her way, including her own daughter.

Those four women laughed together, they cried together, they celebrated, and they cheered each other on. They taught us and continue to teach us, that there are a few basic tenets for life: do the right thing, ALWAYS, even when it sucks. Keep an awesome network of family and friends, and when times get tough, prepare yourself with forgiveness at the ready. Not to mention that relationships are really, really hard. Also, fight aging with everything you got, stand up for yourself and while you're at it, stand up for those who cannot stand up for themselves. If you're prejudiced or bias, get over yourself. Let go and move forward when you have to, but respect yourself and treasure your growth along the way.

Finally, and most importantly, always keep reaching for your dreams no matter how old you are, no matter what hurdles get in the way, especially if the biggest hurdle is yourself.

1

___

WHAT WE DO IN THE SHADOWS

Blanche: I also happen to have a room for rent, and the name is Blanche Devereaux.

Rose: Why would you name a room Blanche Devereaux?

*S*ometime ago I read something along the lines of: "Friendship is the crazy in you recognizing the crazy in someone else and then saying to that person, 'Let's hang out together and share our crazy." It is highly probable I'm not para-phrasing that correctly. It is equally probable that I'm making the whole quote up. Either way, the gist is: friends are awesome because unlike family, we choose our friends. Not that I'm complaining about my family, those people are so crazy they're a hoot. But my friends, those nut jobs are even crazier.

For the GG's, the benefit of picking your friends is that you're able to surround yourself with people who are encouraging, uplift-ing, supportive, and a host of other things that make your daily grind more bearable. Yet, the show makes clear that friendship is something that has to be nurtured and grown and doesn't always come naturally.

In the episode, *The Way We Met,* the audience is shown that the ladies not only didn't immediately hit it off, but they truly kind of loathed each other. Their differences and constant bickering lead all of them to the conclusion that there has to be people with whom they are more simpatico with whom they can live.

Each lady has one foot out the door when Rose introduces the others to cheesecake and story time. As they share dessert she relays a St. Olaf tale about a circus of herrings (which is as ridiculous as it sounds). For Dorothy and Blanche, being regaled with said tale of herring being shot from a cannon provides enough merriment that the ladies are able to see the possibilities of what friendship with one another could bring.

Over the years the cultivation of the friendship among the ladies, as well as the addition of the cantankerous Sophia, is shown to be hard work time and again. However, this theme of friendship is one that, consciously or not, works well with the aforementioned idea of forgiveness. For the GG's their friendship is underlined by their ability to forgive one another which is a moral code we all would do well to live by I'm sure.

The episode, *Hey Look Me Over!* is the story of a mistake in photo development that leads Rose to believe that her beloved husband Charlie once slept with Blanche. Obviously Rose is crushed to think that Charlie cheated on her, but what makes it more devastating is that it happened with her friend. Rose runs a gamut of emotions, but in the end she finds that forgiving Blanche is the only way to move forward.

Of course nobody thought prior to this to look at all of the photos in the pack. It isn't until after the roommates are pals again that Dorothy peruses pictures in the pack and finds all of them to be double exposed. Thus, Blanche and Charlie are exonerated and Blanche is found only to be guilty of using somebody else's camera for a boudoir photo shoot.

Personally, I've never cheated on a friend with a photograph of her husband. This is partly because of my moral code and partly because we don't use real film in cameras anymore. Not to mention - who has the energy to primp and take dirty pics of themselves? There is way too much t.v. that needs to be binged to be fiddling around with a camera. Also, and I have strong conviction in this, I'm pretty sure the Brit would find it more hilarious than sexy if I took boudoir pictures. Hell, I'd probably find it more hilarious than sexy.

I try to maintain healthy friendships with those ladies who I know I can rely on at four in the morning. I want to say I work at my friendships like the GG's do, but in all honesty, I'm not sure that's true. Sometimes, I think you've been friends with someone so long that being friends is almost like a habit or hobby. It is something you do because it's something you enjoy that you've always done. The good thing about friends, as opposed to other habits, is that most of the time you don't have to quit your friends like you do with something like smoking.

Ahhh… smoking. I'm not gonna lie - I loved smoking. Some love drinking, some drugs, and others promiscuous sex with strangers (I was a fan of that too, but I brought my cigarettes with me). For me, the vice du jour was smoking. I loved everything about it. The chronic need to have it in my hand at all times as something to do or have. The taste of the smoke as you inhaled right before it turns to regret and bitterness. The feeling in your chest as it goes down your esophagus. The charring of your lungs from said smoking. The habitual going through the motions, like a bad relationship, because you don't know how to break up with the toxic little suckers that are ruining your life and driving away everyone who loved you. Exhale. Mmmm…. Where was I? Friends! Right…

I try to maintain healthy friendships with those ladies who I know I can rely on for ANYTHING. You know the type, the kind of friend who is so loyal that if you call them at four in the morning and advise that you are outside, in a van, with a bag of lye, a shovel, and the tied up body of your dead husband (I'm not really sure why the husband is tied up in this scenario… in all likelihood I would probably have taken him by surprise in a sudden killing with something like the wok or frying pan. This would be because I just couldn't listen to him tell me how to load the dishwasher "properly" ONE MORE TIME!) they would go with you out to the desert to bury him no questions asked.

In fairness, said friends probably wouldn't help dig, but damn it, they'd hold the flashlight. After the grave is filled in they'd swing into the nearest gas station for a forty of beer and a pack of cigarettes. You would grab the pack of cigarettes and frantically open them, eager to get one in your mouth and start puffing. And in that parking lot of the gas station the two of you would sit silently drinking and puffing in the dark until one of you, usually your companion, breaks the silence with a deep sigh before saying quietly and knowingly, "Dishwasher again?"

At present I have several such friends in my life and of course the no-questions asked desert burial works both ways. I think I might also have this arrangement with a good friend's husband. He's a mumbling low talker and I'm a deaf nodder. So, when we're together he says things and I pretend to hear him, usually by smiling and nodding along. I have warned his wife that if the day comes that he arrives on my porch in a vehicle dripping blood, shovel in hand, that I'm sorry, but I made the commitment to help.

2
___

YOU'RE THE WORST

Rose: Tell me, is it possible to love two men at the same time.

Blanche: Set the scene, have we been drinking?

*I*n the intervening years between getting divorced from husband number one (the Canadian), and marrying husband number two (who we'll lovingly refer to as, The Brit from here forward) I went on a lot of dates. That old saying, "You have to kiss a lot of toads before you find your prince" is nowhere near correct. It's more like, you have to kiss a lot of crap-weasels before you find someone willing to tolerate you and your shenanigans. This is because it's near impossible for us humans to leave our baggage behind for so much of it makes us who we are.

Those scars and memories of our past meld, and out of them comes our steeliness and fortitude. Conversely, it could be we learn fearfulness or inability to trust. Hence, we, the modern female, do not need a prince to come and sweep us off our feet. We need a kind, tolerant, strapping, railway porter capable of lifting said baggage and hauling it wherever we go. Tolerant being key. Forgiveness is super helpful too. And patient - patience is a must.

When I think about my own baggage I realize that while some people's "stuff" is equal to a carry-on, mine is more in the vicinity of the several trunks the Howell's managed to take on that three hour cruise to Gilligan's Island. Why DID they have all that luggage if it was only a three hour tour? And why were they on the tour in the first place? They couldn't afford their own yacht? With so many plot holes they're lucky the Minnow made it to an island instead of sinking.

Anywho.... crap weasels... when I married my first husband my mother tried to warn me, "Never marry a Canadian! Their bacon is ham with an identity crisis and maple syrup is a hard to clean up." It is possible she didn't say that, but it's a good adage to live by just the same.

Years after my divorce it's easier to want to remember my mom warning me about bacon than what she really said which had something to do with us not being right for each other. She hit that on the head. We were sooooo not right for each other. He was much more compatible with the girlfriend he had for the last year of our marriage. They got married a month after our divorce and as far as I know they've lived happily ever after. However, I recently saw a picture of him and let's just say, I feel like I dodged a bullet.

Relationship wise, I wasn't as lucky as the ex to have a new mate built into my next marriage, so after we got divorced I went on the aforementioned scores of dates. Well, it wasn't scores, more like a dozen. And, it wasn't right after the divorce as much as it was three years after the divorce, plus another three years of wallowing in my own crapulence later. So, like six years after the divorce I went on a handful of dates. Well, not dates as much as they were sleep overs. What I managed to learn from these, let's call them encounters, is that dating is hard! Whoever says dating is fun or argues that it is not more painful than a root canal is lying. Or a masochist. Or both. Not that I'm judging.

The GG's were the poster girls for the trials of dating life.

Combined, the four of them must have gone out with all of the eligible bachelors (of a certain age) in Miami. As you might guess, Blanche accounted for the majority of dating in their household, but the others weren't slouches. Dorothy was often teased by her roommates for her dry spells, but she was still a far more prolific dater than most of us today. Even Sophia kept her hand in the dating world with a few boyfriends here and there (I think they were all named Tony), and Rose had at least a dozen short term boyfriends prior to meeting her steady beau, Miles Weber.

Fun fact: Rose actually dated Miles for all of one episode in season one when his name was Arnie - neither of them mentioned that three years later when they met again. Note - Miles was in witness protection and his real name was Nicholas Carbone. Later, we find out he was hiding in Amish country as Samuel Plankmaker. Thus, instead of Arnie being a plot inconsistency it is possible that he was one of Miles' alter egos. We could argue that Rose would have known, but I think we all know that's not necessarily true.

In the cyber age dating isn't really the same as it was in the 80s. On t.v. and movies there is always the meet-cute where the main characters have this adorable encounter. It absolutely does not work this way in real life. These days if you go to a bar with your wingman you find the over forty set looking for their youth, the over sixty set looking to score with a youth, and the under thirty set with their douchy hats and Snidley Whiplash mustaches pretending not to be youth. Actually that's not fair... not all of them wear a hat.

Not being the bar fly type I let my sister convince me that I needed to go the online dating route. First, she conned me into E-Harmony. I spent hours having my will to live sucked down the drain while jumping through all of their hoops only to be told that they didn't have anyone compatible with me for sixty miles. SIXTY miles. That meant that nobody who had signed up for that service within a large populated area of California would find my brand of crazy delightful. The site told me to wait a day or two, matches were on the way. I waited a week and opened up my options to the entire state. Nothing. It wasn't the least bit soul crushing either.

Rather then wait around for a match to be found in a basement somewhere, I ditched the E-Harm and joined a few of the other sites - two paid for and one that was free. Subsequently, like the Golden Girls, I had a few dates with some rather interesting (or dubious) characters. More on that at some other time (ie., when I'm one hundred percent certain my mom is not reading this).

Of the GG's it was Rose who had the most interesting dating life. Dorothy seemed to date a lot schmucks. This is of course with the exceptions of Dick Van Dyke, Leslie Nielsen, Sonny Bono, and the guy from the Carol Burnett Show that wasn't Harvey Korman or Tim Conway. Sophia had the aforementioned Tony's, and Blanche went through a slew of men but never seemed to keep the particularly good ones. Thus, it was Rose whose dates were of note. This is probably because as a person Rose was more accepting and forgiving. It could be boiled down to her naivety or small town ideas, or maybe she was just more open minded than her roommates. However you slice it she was just more apt to date someone who was unconventional than her friends were.

For example: there was Dr. Jonathan Newman. He was a giant in the field of psychiatry. In stature he was a Little Person. Rose was wild about the doc and not only dated him, she pictured herself marrying him. She was aware of the adversity they would have to overcome as well as the public scrutiny that may be put upon their relationship due to their difference in height. However, she believed that their loving relationship could and would conquer all negativity that would be slung their way. In the end that relationship didn't work out, but it was due to Rose not being Jewish rather than Jonathan not being taller.

As the years went by Rose dated a man who thought he was a superhero, a man with impotency issues (she helped him overcome them - talk about a patient woman!), and a con artist after Charlie's pension. At one point she was even accidentally dating a lesbian. To her credit, when she found out, she was kind enough to explain to the woman that had she (Rose) also been gay she would be proud to have such a great person to love.

8

Roses' eclectic romantic capers always played out with an extraordinary amount of heart. That is what essentially made Rose such a lovely character, and Betty White played her with innocence, hilarity, and with warmth. It is easy to mistake Roses' naivety for stupidity, or to think less of her because she wasn't an academic, but that would be missing the point of the character. Rose was symbolic of a universal and forgiving love. She loved not with her eyes or mind, but with her heart and soul which allowed for her to see in others what the shallow care not to see.

As a single lady, I was inspired by Rose and believed I should and could date without being judgmental. I too, could care for others based on who they were on the inside. Turns out I am not quite as gracious a human being as Rose Nylund.

Over the short time that I was in the dating pool I went on a date with a guy who halfway through the meal felt that in the best interest of dinner he should tell me that he had been in prison... like recently been in prison. Like had been released six weeks prior to the date been in prison. I may have slept with him, but it was for research purposes.

On another date I had appetizers with a guy who then took me to help him pick out new work shoes. I didn't sleep with him - his taste in shoes was dreadful. After those two and pre-Brit I was matched with (but didn't meet in person) a very flashy photographer who thought the way to a woman's heart was through his penis.

We hadn't spoke or met, just chatted in that wonderful realm of anonymity that is the internet. Part way through the conversation which was about something as mundane as what we had eaten for lunch, he decided what I really needed was a picture of his genitals.... in his hand... at full mast. After laughing for several minutes I messaged him and advised that I didn't need to see his junk (there may have also been a joke about one in the hand being equal to two in the bush or something like that). I then went on to explain to him that for most women seeing the male genitalia didn't usually have the same effect as female genitalia had for men. Then, in the middle of my diatribe about how female sexuality was more of a combination of things like eyes, sense of humor, kindness, etc. he sent me another pic. So I wished him luck and promptly closed that messenger account. I like to think that the little flasher found a willing recipient of his artistic endeavors. I'm guessing she would be a little like Rose, accepting and kind. And, she would be a lot like Blanche, kinky and dirty.

3

ALL IN THE FAMILY

[Dorothy leaves as Sophia shuts the door and faces Blanche who has been left in charge]

Sophia: Fasten your seat belt, slut puppy!... This ain't gonna be no cakewalk!

Relationships with our (parental) units are tricky. When we are kids we have to follow their rules (I don't know about yours, but mine had a lot). As young adults we are sent out into the great unknown only to find that everything they had said over the years was true and they did know what they were talking about. I don't know about you, but for me, knowing that they were right about most things is particularly annoying. Then, we wake up one day and find that are units are no longer spring chickens. They are getting older which seems to come with its own unique set of challenges.

To their credit, my mother and father are both aging pretty well. At seventy they are both still active, they both still work, and most of the time they seem to still have all of their faculties. A few months back the doctor told my mother that there was no reason why she couldn't make it to a hundred. My mother is skeptical about this, but I'm pretty sure she's got it in it her. I'm less certain my father will make it that long, not because of his health, but rather because one of these days my mom might snap and put an end to him.

As a whole my dad is a pretty adorable old guy. He tootles around with his bff several days a week pretending to be hard at work and he's a legend in his own mind down at the Elk's Lodge. He is getting crankier the older he gets and the fuse for his patience is getting shorter each year. I never thought that fuse was very long to begin with ,so what was maybe two inches has probably been whittled down to less than an inch. It doesn't help that he and my mother both have fiery personalities.

Anyone who has spent any amount with the two of them, especially at their kitchen table, can attest that their sudden outbursts toward one another are a little intimidating (to put it mildly). My sister and I are used to it and don't really notice when they bicker. I don't think they notice when they bicker. Non-veterans of the "flare-ups" are often terrified and will turn to my sister or I with a withering look that implores us to do something. However, we know the rules: Never take a side, and if you do, pray the other sibling takes the side of the other parents so nobody feels ganged up on. That is key.

I told my parents once that I wanted to have little dolls made of them so that someday when they're gone I can reenact their greatest hits. One of my favorite types of their bickering for example is:

Judy (curiously): "Mark, did you cook that egg in oil? You should have used butter."

Mark (a little put out): "Do you want to make breakfast?"

Judy (exasperated): "Oh Timothy Mark! Settle down, I'm just saying, you use butter, not oil for eggs."

Mark (under his breath): "She's talking to me like it's the first time I've ever cooked before (he makes eye contact, you look away so as not to get involved…. Never get involved). She should cook if she doesn't like the way I'm doing it."

Judy (in a half mumble): "I'm just saying, you don't cook eggs in oil. I've never seen anyone cook eggs in oil before. (in a whisper to you) Now the eggs are greasy."

At this point my units will go on like nothing happened, like they didn't just have a hangry spat. The crazy part, however, is not that there can be multiple rounds of spats, but that each lasts under a minute and afterward the two of them are completely fine with one another. If anyone is in trouble after a spat, it's you if you were dumb enough to speak up, make eye contact, or pick a side. In fairness, you were warned. Some people having witnessed these conversations between my parents are astonished that they're not divorced. I think its key to their half century together.

Being married to an Englishman, I find that such behavior doesn't work in our house. The first time I raised my voice at the Brit he stood as still as petrified wood and stared at me, just blinking. I'm not even sure he was breathing. When I was done yelling he looked as though I had skinned his puppy before he strode off gallantly with his head held high saying nary a word to me.

After sulking for a few minutes, I found myself feeling like a heel for being mean to such a sweet and noble creature. So I jetted down the stairs to beg his forgiveness. He did quickly forgave me, and it was two days before I remembered the reason I yelled at him in the first place. The reason I remembered was because he did it again! I can't remember what it was he had done. I just remember wanting to beat him. It was probably because he he advised that he was, "Willing to give a Master Class on dishwasher loading." Freaking dishes.

For years I was caught up in this process where the Brit stepped in it, I "had a go at him" (his words), he did the stoic pout, after which I apologized for being a terrible human being. One day though, I had an epiphany as to what was happening and realized that he was indeed a clever, clever man.

I had been an unwitting pawn in his sick game of "Punk the Wife, Get Out of Trouble." When I confronted him about this he denied it. Then he pouted, and I felt bad. So now I just give him, "The look." This "look" isn't particularly menacing, but it does convey that he's in serious hot water and should he not reverse the situation or his action(s) he might be brutally murdered.

The "look" has come to be the most powerful tool in my marriage arsenal. So I try to use it sparingly so as to not let him get used to seeing it. I wonder if "the look" would ever work on my dad. I've seen my mom give him tons of looks over the years, none of which seemed to stop him in his tracks, which is terrifying because some of her looks could topple governments. She definitely has one in particular that I think she reserves for me alone, and though it may fail to thwart my shenanigans it does give me pause. The older she gets the more I seem to get that look from her.

In the home of the Golden Girls, Dorothy is the keeper of the "looks". As an actress Bea Arthur was capable of conveying everything with just a glance or facial gesture, and she used her abilities well while doing he show. This is especially true when it came to scenes involving her and Estelle Getty's Sophia.

As previously noted, Sophia was a character who defied aging. She was determined to keep living with as much gusto as she could muster and always to the chagrin of her daughter. Like the storyline where Sophia wanted to stay out all night carousing with the senior citizen set. She would go to Roofy's (I think it was a bar, not sure how they spelled it) at all hours and one night didn't bother to come because she "got lucky." Dorothy forbade her to continue such reckless living causing Sophia to choose to move out and live with a super cute, tottering, rich old Englishman (who had no idea who she was).

As a driver Sophia was a menace to society. Yet when Dorothy attempted to take her keys away Sophia just got around her by taking Blanche and Rose's cars. That was kind of the main element in Sophia's playbook - when Dorothy said no she went around her by using Blanche and Rose. Rose in particular was the usual victim of Sophia's ploys and she often found that she had given Sophia money or recourse that Dorothy had previously denied.

I like to think that my parents will continue to age gracefully and defiantly like Sophia. I may have to parent them, or think I am parenting them, but they'll continue to be head strong and sassy. Sophia's in your face dissent from Dorothy's wishes is how I want my units to be when they're her age. Admittedly, I relish the idea of being the one who tells them what they can or can't do, turnabout is fair play. Yet, I equally relish them telling me off and living their lives on their terms.

4

ONE LIFE TO LIVE

[Sophia finishes telling a story] Rose: Wow, Sophia, that was some story!

Sophia: Yeah-funny, touching and with a surprise twist ending. I wonder if was true. Damn that stroke.

$\mathcal{M}$y mother always says that she doesn't mind her birthdays because, "Its better than the alternative." The implication being that the alternative is death (for me, the preferred alternative would be staying at one really good age (like 35) and not getting older). Mom finds that growing older is better than being dead. I'm sure she has a point in there somewhere, but I'm willfully ignoring it. Sure, death is definite and all, but so is aging. Once you're forty you can never be thirty again, and my forty year old knees really miss my thirty year old bod.

As fans of the Golden Girls may know, the roommate with the most trouble aging was Blanche. Ever confident in her own good looks and youthfulness she still struggled with the ongoing mental battle many of us wage against getting older. Not one to shy away from grabbing the bull by the horns, Blanche was even willing to undergo surgery to get the upper-hand on getting older.

In one case, she has a particularly scarring time at a reunion after which she came home resolved to have a face lift. In another, she decided to have her breasts augmented because (and I'm paraphrasing her here) "big bosoms are fashionable again." However, in the end she winds up doing neither of those things and instead of having a "boob job" she donates the money she was going to use for herself so that Sophia's aging friend may live in a nicer, more attentive nursing home. So, what then does it mean for the rest of us when a woman as vain as Blanche forgoes cosmetic enhancements?

Is aging a state of mind or a state of appearance? If it's the former, I'm screwed: my current state of mind is that I'm a forty year old white woman trapped in the body of a ninety year old Sumo wrestler who gave up the job but not the food. But, if we agree that aging is a state of mind, then nobody aged better than Sophia Petrillo.

Throughout the series that woman cooked, she travelled (including a quick turnaround to Sicily to make amends with a spurned lover), she volunteered at the hospital, and frequented her local Senior Center. She was a woman who wasn't afraid of dying so much as she was determined to live her life with gusto.

It would be baffling to Sophia not to give life hell. On more than one occasion she tried to help others follow her lead in accepting that aging wasn't a state of mind or looks, but rather it was a state of doing and being.

In a classic episode titled *Not Another Monday,* Sophia's friend, Martha, is tired of waiting for death and old age to come get her. Rather than dying slowly and painfully from any of an assortment of ailments she didn't yet have, Martha had decided to put an end to things in advance.

Personally, I can't slight Martha for wanting to jump off the train early. I have repeated time and again to my sister and husband: if ever I become terminally ill one, day you'll probably just find me, dead, with a

Post-It note stuck to one hand that reads, "I'm over it." Like Martha told Sophia, "I feel that I don't have the courage to die by inches." Although, does anybody? Do we face dying bravely or is more of a resignation?

In 2016 (the year that music not only died, but died a gruesome death, was pissed on by a hobo and then lit on fire before its remains were swept up and tossed in a urinal) the shocking news came out that David Bowie had died. The media reported that he had been sick with cancer for eighteen months. Yet, two days before his death (and on his birthday no less) he "dropped" a final album. Prior to that he had even filmed a video for a new single and completed a slew of other feats including overseeing the creation of a Broadway play based on his music. I struggle to make coffee in the morning while healthy and Bowie managed to use his last little bit of time on earth to complete more than most of us will in a lifetime.

Somewhere near the close of those eighteen months Bowie had to know that the end was nigh. I can't help but think that he didn't bother with the notion of being brave in the face of death, there was too much left to do before he ran out of time. Recording an album while in the midst of his own demise feels as though Bowie didn't just rage against the dying light (per the Dylan Thomas poem): he grabbed it, used it to light a smoke, and then smashed it with his bare hands. Thus, if life is for living then maybe death is even more so.

I love the idea that upon death we should skip the reflections and admonishing and just be at peace knowing that we had truly lived. Living of course is in and of itself different for each person. For many, if not most people, living is a freedom found in spending time with family and friends. I'm not sure that our definition of having really lived a full life it has to be complicated by what we as individuals have done or whether or not we've been successful, how much money we've amassed, and/or if we're leaving behind some kind of lasting legacy.

Legacy's themselves are a funny thing. There are very few Einstein's, Shakespeare's, and Elvis Presley's in the annals of the world's history. Instead, there are lots of mothers, friends, sons and daughters: nameless and unknown to those whose path theirs didn't cross and for the ones they did, these people were maybe loving, trusting, funny, or wise companions. They were the person on whom someone else counted and loved. Truly isn't that the lasting legacy?

So, what then of Sophia's friend Martha? She died. Well, I'm assuming at some point she died. However, in the episode in question Sophia talked her out of it by promising to be there for her "like a best friend." I wonder if Martha thanked Sophia for being a friend... for traveling down the road and back again? I could on, but it's already in your head so, no need.

5

VAMPIRE DIARIES

"Except for the fact that I've only made love in one position, I've led a very full life." - Sophia

*W*hen I married the Brit, I chose a dress that didn't have sleeves. Initially, I wore a shawl that covered my batwing upper arms... not batwing, that implies a smaller size than they are. I'll try again: Initially, I wore a shawl that covered my Boeing 747 upper arms.

My sister had suggested that maybe I would want to consider wearing a jacket or bridal bolero with it. She wasn't being mean, she just knew that most of my adult life I've had an ongoing war waged against my blubbery arms. My mom, who was sitting alongside my sister that day, said one of the wisest things I've ever heard: "Wear what is comfortable. I don't know why you care about your arms. They're your arms, who cares what anyone else might think?" So, I bought the thin, pretty shawl, wore it through the ceremony and took it off for the pictures.

Today, I rebelliously wear short sleeved shirts in public like a bad-ass and I feel good about it. I walk down the street with my head held high. In my mind the opening riffs to "Stayin' Alive" are playing as I nod to people with a, "That's right, I'm awesome," look on my face. They usually look back at me like, "That fat lady has something wrong with her... she might be demented."

Of course the war I was previously fighting with my arms has now spread to every other part of my body. At some point I guess you just kind of have to give up caring what people might think and accept the fact that for now you're fat and there is no real hiding it. Or at least I did, as there was no real hiding it. A paunchy stomach you can misdirect from with a flowing shirt. With a generous gut, a populous booty and tree-trunk legs, even a muumuu says, "Make room people, I'm coming through!"

Like a lot of others, my adulthood has been spent in one endless, brutal, winner-take-all, prizefight with my body. I blame my mother. If she hadn't cooked delicious comfort food like her spaghetti or homemade mac n cheese maybe I wouldn't like food so much. Truly, this is all her fault. If she had fed me wheatgrass and edamame instead of goulash, I could be a size zero today. My father is culpable too. The man makes the most amazing country gravy with fried chicken remnants. I'm salivating a little just typing about it. I wonder if he's home tonight and what they're making for dinner.

It also doesn't help that I'm a pretty amazing cook myself. Not to brag, but the kitchen is the one place I can frequently nail it. The problem is that I cook so well everything is so delicious when it touches the lips thus, I naturally want more of it. I have, however, learned to circumvent the need for second helpings. I just have one massive helping the first go round. Problem solved.

A few years ago, I taught a Citizenship class at the local adult school. Given that I'm married to a British expat and it was time for him to get his American citizenship I talked him into coming to the class. It was fantastic having him there as the butt of all my Revolutionary War jokes. I frequently cracked myself up mocking his country's inability to take out some farmers with pitchforks. Most of my class didn't speak English very well so they were no where near as amused with me as I was with myself.

When the Brit first came to school I advised the students he was my husband and to feel free to mock him for being English. However, a few of them missed the part about his being my spouse. Over the course of the semester as they realized that he and I were together they were somewhat incredulous that he and I could be married. Being a fair minded, self-loving individual my immediate thought was: "Why can't you believe it? Is it because he's Jack Sprat who could eat no fat and his wife could eat no lean?" Seriously, when we got married he weighed 169 pounds. He's over six three. With his hair he's like six five. I don't say this part about the Jack Sprat to them of course, but I thought it, and when I got home I'm sure I grumbled about it over a donut.

For some of us our self-identity, and by association self-worth, is often tied up in those failings that most bother us. For Rose Nylund a lot of her self image rested in who she really was. Rose was the type of character who was always a chipper chicken and seemingly free of self-doubt, self-effacement, and self-pity. That is until we learn that she was adopted and had spent her entire life living with the day dream that her biological father was Bob Hope. She knew in her heart that he wasn't really her father, but something in her loved something about him so much she held onto the childhood notion that he could be.

I think a lot of us secretly wonder who it is that we truly are. For example: Am I really a middle aged, twice married (neither time to an American), former social-worker who now teaches at an Adult School? If so, what the heck does that mean? Honestly? It means nothing, absolutely nothing. That's because who I am has nothing to do with where I work or how I look (which is actually probably a good thing because I can't remember the last time I put on make-up).

The other day a student asked me if I've been sick. I replied, "Is it because I'm not wearing make-up?" Chagrinned, he admitted that was indeed the case. He flunked his math test that day.

As for loving what we do, I feel like it's probably safe to say that a greater portion of the population does not do what they love for a living. I do, and my sister does, but outside of us, and maybe a few other people I know everyone else just works to make money so that they can do or have whatever it is they want. Therefore, what we do can't possibly be entangled in who we are. I'm sure that very few tombstones have, "Bob Smith, retired from the phone company after happily climbing poles for thirty years." Most tombstones have a variation of, "Loving wife," "Loving Mother" or something along those lines on them.

I also question the idea that those titles such as "loving sister" define us. I am a loving sister, but also a wife, an ex-wife, a daughter, a niece, a co-worker, and a friend. But being in these relationships don't make me who I am. Having them do. For me, this is especially true of the relationship with my sister.

As far as relationships go, outside of the one with my parents and my marriage to the Brit, the one with my sister has been the most important in my life. My other roles in life have been important too, but maybe not as defining as sister-hood. As long as she is alive, my sister will always be that one person on the planet who has shared childhood experiences with me. She is the only other person who truly gets it when I say, "Dude, your mother is crazy." She knows exactly the crazy I'm talking about.

I'm certain that all children think their moms are at one time or another "crazy." You know, it's that something a mother does or says that makes her children go, "WTF is wrong her?" with a heavy eye roll and sometimes an accompanying deep sigh. Yes, *THAT* crazy. To which I am referring Thus, my sister is the one who totally knows what I mean when I talk about *our* mother's particular kind of crazy.

Through the years my sister and I have had many, many MANY fights and often have relished in getting the other one in trouble with the units. But, we also have been each other's pals and confidantes. Part of who I am is due to my relationship with her. She constantly is on me to do better, to be better. It's actually pretty annoying.

When I used to smoke she would hound me all the time about

quitting. She would go so far as to tell me how she will have to put my urn on her mantle so she can continue to lecture me long after I've died of lung cancer. Because, you know, I'm going to die of lung cancer. She drives that point home, hard. Being the stubborn older sibling, I would refuse to listen to her, but, in the end I quit and I begrudgingly give her the victory.

When I'm a jerk (and this happens more often than not), she's the one person willing to call "shenanigans" on me and she implores me to at least attempt to be a better human being. When I comply it's really only because I don't want to hear her lecture me again. Come to think of it, most of my decisions are based on how willing or not, I am to listen to her in the event I get caught doing something for which she is going to lecture.

As for Rose, she did come to terms with the fact that Bob Hope was definitely not her biological father. Turns out it was Don Ameche. For those of you who don't know who Don Ameche is I refer you imdb.com, and really, you should be ashamed of yourself.

Upon finally meeting her bio dad, said Don Ameche, who incidentally was a monk, Rose was able to realize that she had had a great life in spite of not knowing him. She also realized that she knew who she was - she was Rose Nylund - an orphan adopted into an awesome family. She was someone who had had a great childhood, an awesome marriage, good kids, and a fairly charmed life. The moral to the story? It's not our biology, our jobs, or our facades that define us. It's those lifelong relationships with people who were trapped in the same hostage situation with us that do.

6

PARENTHOOD

[to Dorothy] "Come here. Sometimes a mother gets a little busy and forgets to tell her daughter everything she needs to know. So I'm telling you now. Don't date a priest, it's bad luck. Trust me on this one." - Sophia

$\mathcal{U}$nless you count too many cats, two box turtles (one of which is missing), a Brit, and an unruly old Basset Hound my parenting experiences are limited to men and pets. Sometimes the two haven't been mutually exclusive. Thus, I don't know a ton about parenting. Yet, if raising a child is anything like trying to herd a Basset Hound into behaving as a productive citizen in society, I'm not sure I'm cut out for it; the dog alone is exhausting and causes a great amount of mental anguish. I couldn't imagine mini humans being any less so.

This hound dog who plagues me is actually not mine alone. He also belongs to my sister who was living with me following the end of my first marriage and prior to the start of her first one. Yeah, we both have been married twice. My parents who have been together for nearly fifty years are so proud.

So, when Quincy the Basset Hound first arrived in our lives (via our aunt who used to breed Bassets) it was on a bright and warm Easter Sunday. We were in our aunt's yard and before us was not one litter of odiferous, rollie-pollie Basset puppies, but two. They were enclosed in this cute little makeshift play-pen and there was some ungodly number of them-like, fourteen or fifteen. My sister had always wanted a Basset Hound - one she could name Melvin and pull along in a Radio Flyer.

I tried to have no part of what I felt was going to be a travesty: I already had 2 large mongrels and four cats at home (these are different cats than the ones previously mentioned) and I was determined to hold fast to my definitive "no" on the puppy. I was unyielding for all of 30 seconds.

Being as that we were dealing with puppies, and a plethora of them at that, over a dozen little noses were sniffing at us through their enclosure while tails wagged and puppy whines beseeched the air. If you have never seen a swarm of Basset Hound puppies you should know that they are the cutest of all puppies bar none. Sure, others breed are adorable, but with those round bellies, big paws, short stature, and super awesome long ears, Bassets have that little something extra that other types are missing. It could be that they all smell like corn meal, I don't know how or why, but they do. All Bassets smell like corn meal and sweat. And maybe a little like a dumpster.

We spent what felt like hours scratching a little guy here and petting another there, going the rounds to give them each a chance to be ours when suddenly - HE appeared. Atop the other dogs leapt the fattest, most cuddly and captivating pile of odor I've ever seen or smelt. His eyes locked with ours and it was love at first squeal, ours, not his.

Quickly, he body surfed over his siblings and cousins and you could tell he would have been there sooner if he hadn't been napping in the food bowl. He tripped over his long ears a couple of times, but still, he persisted until he was able to take two good leaps and pounce, face first, right into the side of pen.

With haste we snatched him up and declared him the love our

lives. Quickly we christened him, Quincy Melvin Satchel Howard Taft III. Then and there we took him home and so began the single greatest night of hell I or my sister had experienced (up to that point in our lives).

He was too small to let run amok in the house, and he wasn't potty trained. The big dogs I had already weren't sure what they thought of him One of my dogs kept looking at him as though she figured he would make a great amuse bouche. So, to be safe, we put him in the bathroom for the night.

From behind that door he whined, he scratched, he howled, he barked, he relieved himself on the floor (and not on the puppy pad provided), and he really went out of his way to ensure that nobody in the neighborhood was sleeping that night.

At work the next day I was wallowing in my crapulence when I received an email from my sister stating that we needed to take Quincy Melvin Satchel Howard Taft III back to our aunt. My brain, bloodshot eyes, and langover (that's a hangover from lack of sleep) agreed, yet, for some unknown reason, I told her no. I gave her some lecture on how she wouldn't be able to send a crying human baby back if she had one, therefore she needed to figure out how to parent her little bundle of misery. She didn't really argue with me, which to be honest - she always did. Arguing is her forte. At least arguing with me is.

So, I was genuinely surprised when she came home that night with a baby gate for our kitchen, a ginormous crate, a stuffed bear, and a dog bed. I was really impressed. She was determined that she was going to thwart the monster we had adopted and turn him into a delightful animal. It's occurring to me as I write this that's probably how my mother felt when I was a child. Maybe that's how every parent feels?

Over on the Golden Girl's that might be how Blanche's kids felt about her. In several episodes Blanche admitted to her friends that as a young mother she left her kids in the care of nannies, citing her own selfishness as motivation for doing so. She wanted to be young, social, and carefree, not stuck at home being a mother. Subsequently, six of her children, and especially her daughters, Janet and Rebecca, had significant resentment toward her.

Janet's mother/daughter relationship with Blanche is such that near the conclusion of an episode where Blanche had considered adopting a baby left at their house (long story, Rose was involved) she calls Janet just to "chat." We're not privy to Janet's responses to her mother but can infer from Blanche's words that they are not positive ones. It would seem that Janet was even perplexed as to why her mother was contacting her.

In another episode, centered on Mother's Day, the audience waits in semi-anguish with Blanche to see if Janet is going to call her. The phone has rung throughout the day as the ladies reminisced and told stories, yet Blanche notes that she has yet to hear from her daughter and indicates a deep hope that she will even though she doesn't really expect to. When the phone finally rings and Blanche excitedly sighs Janet's name in relief the participating audience probably can't help but be relieved as well.

The relationship between Blanche and Rebecca is maybe not as strained as the one with Janet, yet it's not exactly on solid footing either. I should note: I'm referring to the relationship Blanche had with the second Rebecca. The first Rebecca was portrayed in season three as an overweight, former model engaged to a verbally abusive creep.

Inevitably, Blanche helps Rebecca to see her self worth and by the episode's end the odious fiancee has been kicked to the curb. When we next meet Rebecca she is model thin again and portrayed by a completely different actress. Blanche also had two different men playing her father, Big Daddy. Before DVRs show runners were able to get away with a lot more than they do today. In this regard, the case of the two Darrin's on Bewitched should serve as adequate evidence.

So, second Rebecca's trips to Miami allowed for the development of a new, adult connection with her mother. She challenges Blanche's sensibilities by choosing to be artificially inseminated and is intent on raising the child by herself. Blanche, the modern day

Casanova, is decidedly old fashioned in a number of matter including child rearing. She believes that a child needs both a mother and a father and apparently a nanny or two. The back and forth between her and Rebecca as they try to hold onto their bond while having markedly separate views feels like an authentic portrayal of the dynamics between mothers and their kids.

That's not to say that all mother-child relationships are strained, but many are wrapped in a subconscious (and sometimes conscious) pact whereby we as the children, know that they, the parents, are constantly assessing (judging) our life choices so that they can guide us toward the best outcome (ie. tell us where we went wrong and how we could have avoided that if we had just listened to them in the first place).

It's interesting to note that through the first Rebecca and other overweight characters that appear on the show, we see all of the understanding and compassion that is usually reserved for characters who struggle within society (whether due to their sexual orientation, age, or skin color) completely evaporate.

Apparently the writer's of the show had no tolerance for people who had weight issues. This is evident via their fat jokes that are lampooned at Rebecca mostly using Sophia as the mouthpiece. The aforementioned horrid fiancee mocks Rebecca for her weight as well, but you're supposed to expect it from him because he's a louse. It feels though that Sophia jerk attitude toward the overweight is to be forgiven because she had a stroke and can't control her inner monologue. Both seem like perfect excuses to pick on the obese.

When Sophia meets Rebecca she says to her, "You're Blanche's daughter, the model?" She then turns to Dorothy and Rose to mutter, "What'd she model, car covers?" Given Sophia's progressive views on equality, race relations, and gay love one would expect her to have a similar stance toward those with weight issues. Yet, like all of us, Sophia is the victim of her own ideologies. Sadly this is most evident when it comes to her son, Phil Petrillo.

Like Vera on Cheers or Maris on Frasier, Phil Petrillo was one of

...ose characters that you so oft heard about, but never got to lay eyes on. Since childhood he had plagued Sophia with his desire to dress in women's attire. As an adult he continued to cross-dress. Additionally, he married a woman Sophia detested. Together they had ten children, none of whom graduated high school, and the entire family lived in a trailer. Phil was completely misunderstood by his mother who blamed herself for his being what she called, "Different."

> **Rose Nylund:** [about Phil] So what if he was different? It's okay that you loved him.

> **Sophia Petrillo:** [voice cracking] I did love him. He was my son, my little boy. But every time I saw him I wondered what I did, what I said, when was the day I did whatever I did to make him the way he was.

> **Angela Petrillo:** [tenderly] What he was, Sophia, was a good man.

Sophia frequently cracked jokes about Phil. Maybe it was to assuage her own discomfort with him. Angela, however, loved him for who he was and when he passes away suddenly in season six she goes head to head with Sophia to ensure that Phil's memory isn't tarnished by his mother's inability to understand him.

Conversely, Dorothy seems more comfortable with her brother's cross-dressing (though she appears somewhat unnerved by Phil being buried in a black teddy), even reminiscing during her eulogy for him that her favorite memories included she and he dressing up like the Bronte sisters when they were children.

I'm not sure why Phil was buried in Florida when he was always mentioned as having lived in New York. Nor am I sure why none of his ten kids nor his sister Gloria were there for the funeral when in mention of him in other episodes it seemed as though he was believed by all.

Come to think of it, in an episode from season one when

Dorothy tells Sophia not to argue with Phil's wife when she goes Brooklyn for a visit Sophia replies, "We get along okay. Phil's wife has her good points. She's sweet, she's reliable, and when her father gets out of prison she'll be a wealthy woman!" Maybe I'll just refer us back to the previous aside regarding the two Rebeccas and the two Big Daddy's and leave it at that.

Thus, although Sophia didn't always understand her son, she does make the case in multiple episodes that she had affection for him noting, "I love all my children... even Phil." I wonder if she would have loved Quincy?

After my sister came home with the arsenal of dog training supplies that second night he became one spoiled pup. Each evening for the first year of his life he was put to bed in his crate after having been regaled with stories of brave canines rescuing princesses and slaying dragons. He was tucked in with a dish towel warmed in the microwave and snored loudly, head on his teddy bear, to a playlist of music we made him. He doesn't get a personal stream of lullabies anymore, but he still snores. And, he still smells like corn meal. And sweat. And a dumpster.

---

* Note: Quincy passed away before this book was published. At twelve years and eight months old we lost him during emergency surgery to remove cancerous tumors. Not a day goes by that I don't miss him and pretend to hear him snoring near by.

7

AWKWARD

"She happens to like girls instead of guys. Some people like cats instead of dogs. Frankly, I'd rather live with a lesbian than a cat. Unless the lesbian sheds, then I don't know." - Sophia

The other day a student asked me if it was possible that her grandson who is gay "became that way" because she watched gymnastics with him when he was a kid. I asked her to clarify. She then said, "I used to watch gymnastics with him when he was a kid, did that turn him gay?" I honestly didn't know how to respond without slapping her silly so I took a deep breath, quickly prayed for patience, and then explained biology to her

I find it strange that there are still those people out there who believe that a gay person can be "turned" gay. It is in the same ideological camp as homosexuality or gender identity being a choice. If this were true, nobody in their right mind would make such a choice for it would be the same as choosing to be discriminated against, shunned by other members of society, ridiculed, belittled, and bullied, and so much more.

Nobody in their right mind is going to choose to live a life involving that much struggle. However, people have chosen to join the Nazi's and Neo-Nazi's. People have chosen to drop atomic bombs. People have chosen to wipe out beautiful species of animals from the face of the earth due to the choice to ignore climate science. People choose to be biased, ignorant, and cruel. It is remarkable that frequently such choices go unpunished.

The hunters who wiped out the native Buffalo weren't imprisoned for their actions but the wonderful playwright Oscar Wilde was because he loved men. How does that make sense? Alan Turing helped the Allies to win World War II. His reward? He was outed as a homosexual and chemically castrated subsequently leading him to take his own life.

What then does it say about the human condition that many Nazi's who took part in the Holocaust weren't imprisoned or hung for their crimes, yet throughout the world today people are still imprisoned for their sexual preferences?

An uncle of mine used to always say to us kids (and it's highly probable he swiped it from Rodney King's televised plea for an end to the '92 LA Riots), "Why can't we all just get along?" Or more simply put by Sophia Petrillo, "Everyone wants someone to grow old with and shouldn't everyone have that chance?"

When put in simple terms the desire to love and be loved should be universally understood and accepted. Bias, however, continues to be prevalent in this world. Whether it be toward people's sexual preferences, the color of their skin, their religion (or lack thereof), and any other of a multitude of baseless reasons prejudice remains an underlying ill in our society.

Each of the GG's had prejudices and biases that they had to surmount through the course of the show. The fact that these fierce characters were shown as being incredibly strong and yet also capable of a human depravity is perhaps what allows for the show's influence and popularity to continue to thrive.

Dorothy's son wanted to marry an older black woman. Dorothy didn't oppose because the bride to be she was black, but rather because she was a lot older (of course if we delve into continuity nd the show's own lack of comprehensiveness we would remember that her son should actually be in his forties and not the twenty-three she claimed him to be, thus, his bride's age is a moot point). On the other hand, Sophia, wasn't opposed to the marriage at all. She and the bride's grandmother each understood that getting between young lovers would have no good outcome.

Now, where Sophia was pretty hip and socially aware, Blanche was the complete opposite. The one issue that probably plagued her the most, however, was her misunderstanding of and bias toward homosexuality (and that's not counting her confusing lesbians with the Lebanese). Unaware of her latent prejudices, Blanche was faced with them when her brother Clayton came out to her and her room-mates. Clayton had always been known to his sister as a "ladies man" and she falsely believed that he had chased as many skirts through the years as she had slacks. Upon receiving the truth, that Clayton had been feigning his interest in women in order to fit in, Blanche is dumbfounded and willfully refuses to believe it. It's not with malicious intent that Blanche won't accept her brother's truth about being gay. Rather, she is the victim and perpetrator of a deep rooted willful ignorance.

Having never had to walk a mile in his shoes, Clayton's previous societal choices such as getting married to a woman, seemed to prove to Blanche that Clayton is wrong about his own sexuality. Blanche can't comprehend why her brother would be anything other than himself, but that is based on her idea that "himself" should be heterosexual.

Blanche honestly does not seem to grasp that many people go through life having to hide their true selves. She believes everyone is like her, what you see is what you get. Yet her un-enlightened state and ignorance is perhaps indicative of her upbringing. Her family seems to have had a general latent intolerance for anything not within the confines or their societal norms.

Why do humans feel we have an entitlement as to how or who somebody else loves? Or even how somebody else believes (or not), lives (or not), thinks (or not)? That always perplexes me. The fact that there had to be a fight, a long emotionally fraught struggle, for LGBTQ people to have the right to get married is baffling. Who has the time and emotional wherewithal that it takes to actively seek to bar another person from being who they are or living how they want? I don't have the energy most days to get out of my pajamas let alone lead a crusade to prohibit a percentage of the population from expressing their love like the rest of us.

Maybe that's just it - maybe, it's that some of us think we know what's best for all of us and that continues to fuel the bigotry still thriving in the world today. Our inability to accept other's differences is perhaps more of a reflection of our own failure to break from the herd than it is a rejection of their failure to assimilate. Or maybe, like Blanche, it has to do with appearances.

It should be noted that by the end of Clayton's first episode on the show all is improved and we find that Blanche is choosing to love her brother for who he is rather than ostracize him for not being who she wants. Well, sort of. Two seasons later she receives a letter from Clayton saying that he has big news to share with her about which she says, "I bet I know what the surprise is… Clayton's met himself a girl, and he wants me to meet her." When Dorothy chastises her she responds with, "Dorothy, I think that gay thing was just a phase he was going through."

Subsequently, Clayton arrives with his fiancee, Doug, and we, the audience, are privy to how nonsensical Blanche can be (and Rose is the dumb one?). She even says to her friends: "I don't really mind Clayton being homosexual, I just don't like him dating men…there must be homosexuals who date women?" Sophia explains to her that there are; "They're called lesbians."

Typical of Blanche's reaction to, or rather her over-reaction to things, she admonishes Clayton for wanting to marry Doug and tries to persuade him to realize what people will think of her should he marry a man.

It is often that way for Blanche - she has an ongoing obsession with what others may think of her based on the actions of someone else entirely. She's okay with her own reputation as a wanton slut, e's quite proud of that. However, when Rebecca (the slim curly haired Rebecca not the chubby straight haired one) wants to have a baby by artificial insemination Blanche's feelings toward her daughter's choice stem from what others might think about her (Blanche) having a daughter who is an unwed mother.

Ever the narcissist, Blanche fails to take into account that it's simply not about her, it's about the other person and who they are or what they want for their lives.

Thus, this is one of the great failing of humans - we spend so much time worried about what others might think about us that we don't use our heads. We care so much for the opinions of strangers that we fail the people who do love us by not considering how they feel, what their experiences are, or what validation they might need in any moment of their life. If we could but remember that nobody outside of our circle of loved ones is really thinking about us at all then we can focus instead on supporting and respecting everyone and not just ourselves.

8

ANGER MANAGEMENT

"Wait a minute, let me get this straight. We lived with a filthy pig in our house, bought a whole bunch of stuff on credit we can't afford, and now we're gonna kiss off 100,000 bucks because the pig is homesick? Sometimes life really bites the big one." - Sophia

ollowing the unexpected death of her husband George, Blanche made a point of putting up barriers in relationships. She couldn't take herself out of the dating pool, her libido was too prolific for that, however, when faced with matters of the heart she struggled to be vulnerable. George's death left her with a wound that she was adamant not to experience again.

Rose, on the other hand fell for the college professor, Miles, and enjoyed the pleasures that can come from an intimate relationship. However, she too struggled with the idea of fully giving herself to the new relationship. Over the course of several episodes throughout the series' run each woman battled with the idea of letting go and moving forward. "Letting go"as it were proved time and again to be something of a consistent and recurring process that was incredibly hard for the GG's to do.

It probably goes without saying that the concept of letting go (or moving forward) is different for everyone. My extremely uptight English husband is completely unable to relax or let things go. He gets twisted into balls of frustration and anxiety when he needs to move on and put something behind him. It is as though he is physically incapable of allowing himself to be mentally free of things that are bothering him.

He asked me once, "Dear, how would one go about the letting go of something if they were so inclined?" I thought it over and then told him, "You just do." He blinked at me from across the table with a look that seemed to convey that he was not impressed with my answer. Still, he trudged on: "Sure, but HOW do you let it go?" I knew the man really needed an answer and I didn't want to let him down. I dug really deep into the confines of my mind for a plausible answer: "You make the conscious choice to not let the matter affect you anymore." He told me I was fired.

Later that week on the show *Big Bang Theory*, Sheldon was also having a difficult time with letting something go. Penny helped by advising him to imagine his problem as a pen and then to essentially drop the pen as a symbolic letting go (naturally there was more to it than this since Sheldon was involved, but that's a different story). The Brit paused the t.v. as we watched this scene, turned to me and said, "Why didn't you explain it like that?" Insert exasperated deep sigh accompanied by an eye roll here.

In a sad, yet very sweet and poignant episode of the Golden Girls Blanche's brother-in-law, Jamie, comes to Miami. The two enjoy a light hearted meal which for her seems to ignite old romantic feelings. Believing that she's falling in love with him, Blanche embarrasses herself by professing feelings for Jamie who doesn't feel the same. Luckily for her, Jamie realized Blanche didn't love him but rather it was her old feelings for George being projected on to him. Kindly, he told her, "You're in love with the memory of George I've brought back to you." Heart broken, but knowing that it was true, Blanche concedes before locking herself in her room to yet again mourn her lost love George.

Marital relationships frequently appear as a theme through the show. With Dorothy and Stan the lesson was usually about forgiveness, yet in *Stan Take a Wife* (from season four) Dorothy finds herself in the awkward position of having to let Stan go.

Given his history of being a schmuck it should be easy for Dorothy to fork him over to his intended, Katherine. However, prior to his nuptials Stan uses force in a stand off at the hospital over Sophia's well being. This act of aggression and chivalry from Stan reminds Dorothy of those times in their marriage when he wasn't causing her grief but rather made her proud. Subsequently, she makes the decision to stop his marriage to Katherine so that she might be with him again. Luckily for her, she revealed her intentions to her friends who were thoughtful enough to put an end to her scheming.

In the end, Dorothy has an anonymous encounter with Katherine (in the bar of the hotel where the wedding is taking place) and discovers a lovely woman who earnestly loves Stan. This meeting illustrates for Dorothy the folly in her sabotage idea and she capitulates having to let go not only of the idea of being with Stan but also of Stan her hero so that he may create a new life with another. It is Stan though (if you know the show, you know what I mean) so ultimately the marriage to Katherine doesn't work out and Dorothy once again finds herself to be the main woman in his life (whether she likes it or not).

Letting go is something we all probably feel should be inherently easy, yet most of us find it to be incredibly challenging. The Brit is so bad at letting things go that I saved the song "Let it Go" from *Frozen* onto my phone. This is so I can play it at him each time he spirals on some psychotic rant I've heard before about some problem that is virtually non-existent. It's easier to hit play on the phone than listen at this point.

You might think I'm a terrible wife who isn't meeting my spouse's emotional needs, but you don't understand how crazy his problems usually are. For example: a recent repetitive issue of his was lack of space at work. Throughout an entire summer there were

...ess ravings about his department being unappreciated. This ...as backed up by his favorite go to statement, "How could they be expected to work with no space!"

The Brit had his own office, but he had taken up most of the square footage by putting his desk smack dab in the middle of the area so as not to have his back to the door or the window. He does this wherever he has a desk (including at home) as he has an innate need to not be taken by surprise in the event of a zombie apocalypse. His department actually had a few offices and an entire room for materials related to their job activities. Yet, he was imminently close to quitting said job after having to suffer the humiliation of "no space" which to most can only be described as inane.

In an attempt to create space via squatting in other departments' territories the Brit and a co-worker forcibly acquired some cabinets for their stuff by literally placing said stuff in and around said cabinets.

When the department who had previously had rights to the cabinets (prior to the aforementioned squatting) asked the Brit if he would mind moving his departments' stuff just long enough for the first department to remove their things the Brit and Co. were of course incensed.

Though their cabinets were taken out from under them the folks from the other department chose not to fight, but rather just to remove their office supplies and let the cabinets go. Yeah, I'm not making this up.

So, it's not that I'm a mean wife, it's that I'm a long suffering wife who for three months was plagued by the "space rant" of a nutter. In the end his company got his department new, BIGGER offices and he was finally happy. Two weeks later he started working remotely from home. I'm imagining a pen....

9

THE GOOD WIFE

"People waste their time pondering whether a glass is half empty or half full. Me, I just drink whatever's in the glass." -Sophia

In the fifth season of the Golden Girls' Blanche Devereaux (played so superbly by Rue McClanahan) finds out that her beloved dead husband, George, sired a son with another woman. Not only that, but said son showed up on her doorstep years after George's untimely death wanting to know about his father. As any red blooded woman would be, she was outraged.

Having spent years living with fond memories of the only man to whom she was faithful (as you may know, for Blanche that was a big deal) she was suddenly left with a mixed image of him and more importantly with questions to which she would never have the answer: Why or how could he do such a thing? Was it serious or a fling? Did he know she turned down sleeping with Andy Rooney while they were married?

Her friends, ever the comfort in times of grief, came to her aid with pearls of wisdom. Dorothy offers two different theories: 1) Men are, as she says, "Victims of the evolutionary process which genetily programs their sexual habits." And 2), "Men are scum." Sophia's sage words of advise were to speak of a time when her Sal nearly cheated on her with a mouthy "bird of a thing," while she was pregnant with her son Phil and "crying all the time." Rose urged Blanche to look beyond George's actions and forgive him saying, "Don't throw away all the good memories just because of a mistake."

Forgiveness appears to be a major theme throughout the show's run. It was second in importance only to friendship. In countless episodes one or more of the main characters come to a point where they need to seek the forgiveness of another person. In many cases Rose, Dorothy, and Blanche find themselves hat in hand with each other over some sort of row or slight: Dorothy and Blanche read Rose's diary. Rose forgave them. Blanche was mad that Rose allegedly slept with Blanche's brother (she didn't, he's gay). Rose forgave her. Dorothy kisses Miles, Rose's steady beau of the last two seasons of the show. Rose forgave her. Sophia lied to Dorothy when she was a teenager about her prom date ditching her. Dorothy forgave her.

By and large, more time might have been spent on the characters seeking absolution than eating cheesecake. Seems impossible doesn't it? And yet, it's true. Well, maybe it's true. I didn't actually count how many times they ate cheesecake before comparing it to how many times they had to apologize. I maintain, however, that there was a lot of penance going on. So much so there were even two episodes featuring priests.

What then does it mean for our silver foxes that so much of their stories were tied up in their exonerations? Perhaps this was to illustrate what horrible and unjust people these characters really were that they would do these horrible in the first place. Or, maybe it was so that these characters could not just learn and grow, but also show how fallible we as humans truly are. Every mistake, every misplaced step or hurtful remark was part of an education for the rest of us.

Dorothy for whatever reason was most often in the role of the forgiver, rather than the forgiven. This was due in part to her having been married to Stan Zbornak.

Long after their divorce, Stan continued to be a major part of Dorothy's life and along with his presence inevitably came the need for his apologies.

In the beginning (and by beginning I mean the second episode of the series) Stan returns for the wedding of his and Dorothy's daughter, Kate. With the wounds of the divorce still fresh, Dorothy has a difficult time just having him in the same house as herself. More than once her friends had to thwart her from strangling him (this is also a recurrent theme). Yet, by the end of the episode, after she tells him what she thinks of him, she begins to forgive him. Importantly, she doesn't let her feelings toward him stop her from relaying a heartfelt message about the goodness of marriage to her daughter when Kate suffers from pre-wedding jitters. Oh, by the way — later in the series we find out Kate's husband cheats on her too. But, as Sophia would say, that's a different story.

Repeatedly, we find Dorothy and Stan engaged in an intense battle for her forgiveness of him. She also sleeps with him, a lot. That probably doesn't do much to help her confused feelings toward him.

These two characters are perpetually locked in what can only be deemed a stalemate: he screws up and after reading him the riot act, she forgives him. Maybe the Zbornaks work as a metaphor for marriage by embodying the give and take that comes with sharing your life with another person.

We can't all be saints all of the time and when we fail or fall it's usually the person (or persons) to whom we're closest that suffer the consequences with us. I don't know if it's an innate human need to make those who love us proud of us or to somehow be worthy of love, but most of us do keep trying to do and be better. We stumble, we get up, we fight on and the one thing that can mean the most when we do make a mess of things is the forgiveness and understanding of our loved ones.

Without forgiveness what does life mean? It would instead be an xistence whereby when we fail or fall we have no need for improvement. Let's face it, each of us left to our own devices has little motivation to do or be good. Like the old adage says: if a dog craps on the sidewalk and there is nobody there to scoop it up how many people walk through it and get it on their good shoes? The moral of course being that we're all the pooping dog and the rest of the world is the shoes. So, without someone caring enough to help clean up our messes through their love and compassion we just continuously crap on everybody else. But back to Blanche…

Blanche makes the decision to follow Rose's advice and forgive George. Beyond that, she lets the illegitimate son, David, into her home and shares pictures and stories of George with the young man. She chose to exonerate George of his sin against her.

I'm not advocating that we all forgive adulterous husbands (or wives, or what-have-you), that's something I'm sure has to be on a case-by-case basis. As Dorothy can attest, divorce and cheating spouses are really hard on the ego. Blanche's ego wasn't unscathed by the revelation of George's infidelity, that's a hurt she would always have going forward, but she chose to forgive him not for his benefit, but for her own. In the end we have to take care of those we love, but we equally need to take care of ourselves.

PART TWO

In December of 2018 my father was diagnosed with Stage 4 cancer that had metastasized to his brain creating one super large mega tumor in the middle of both brain lobes. The news was incredibly devastating for us all. The physicians tried valiantly to save him, and he was improving, however, the tumors were too aggressive and he wound up passing on February 24, 2019. The following chapters were completed following his death.

10

LIFE IN PIECES

Dorothy: It's so hard to dress for a psychiatrist. You wear black, they think you're depressed. You wear red, they think you're angry.

Blanche: You wear a negligee, they think you want to sleep with them.

Dorothy: Why aren't you arrested more?

I find it immensely difficult to be a witness to my mom's broken heart. There is a helplessness in not being able to do anything, at all for someone I love who is in pain. I can't make it better - I haven't figured out how to bring my father back. I've thought of a few ways we could try to do so, but my sister keeps telling me no. All the while, I know that my mom's grief is so heavy, she must not be able to breathe at times. She keeps a brave face and tries not to cry in front of anyone, but we know it's there, looming in the background. My uncle used to always say that nobody can feel our pain like we feel our pain . I never truly knew what he meant until now.

Last year, before my father's passing, but after he had been diag-

nosed, a good friend of mine and I were having lunch. Her o
father had been in the hospital for a possible stroke. As we ate an
talked about our respective fathers she said something to the effect
of, "I never thought about us being that age where our parents were
old enough to die." Neither had I. How many people do?

I had never thought about being forty let alone my parents being
seventy or my dad getting cancer. Is it a conscious thing to think of
the mortality of our loved ones? Are some folks just always aware
that they, and subsequently their parents, or others, are aging?

My dad was so vibrant. He could be a pain in the butt, but he
was also a lovely human being. He was that larger than life character who everyone loved. There wasn't anyone he wouldn't help,
from the guy on the street needing a few bucks, to the kitten
dumped in a trash can that he took home and raised. He was this
beacon of light and warmth, so it was devastating to us all for that
light to be extinguished - and most of all to my mom.

Mom had spent nearly fifty years living with the guy. I get a little
weirded out being alone when the Brit is gone for the night. I would
hate to have to figure out how to live alone again. But at least I've
done it before. My mom hasn't.

Thanks to the divorce from the Canadian I knew what it was like
to have your world upturned and to go from an existence with
which you were familiar — and even liked - to having to do something else entirely. Like my mom's new life, it was an existence I
didn't get a vote in. So, that part about being alone, the part about
being left abruptly by the spouse and having to start over - I understood that part.

I also understand being sad, I'm sad too. What I can't grasp is
the idea that for her, the person she had spent the last fifty years
looking at, fighting with, loving, eating meals with, vacationing
with, raising a family with... for her, that person was gone.

I actually still can't fathom that he's gone at all and it's been over
nine months and am actively resisting accepting that he's no longer
here. I am finding that living in constant denial feels like a really
good place for me mentally. Dad ran his own vending business and

s always out and about, going to his client's respective places of usiness and fixing things. In my mind, he's just been off repairing a jukebox that is irreparably broken.

On the other hand, my mother and sister are determined to be adults about things and are proactively dealing with their grief head on (insert an eye roll and heavy sigh of semi-disgust here).

Apparently, part of that whole being mentally healthy thing is facing the loss. What they don't realize though, is that I'm going to outwit conventional science. Muhahahaha! I was a social worker for CPS for a long time - I can drive anything down, deep. Like tunneled into the Earth's core heading for the inner sanctum where the lizard people deep. Is it lizard people? Mole people? Either way - *deep*.

The other trick up my sleeve is that I also can do a really job of ignoring things. Ask the Brit - I ignore him at least once a week for a good half hour. To be fair, it's only when he's on his weekly rant about the sizes of iPhones and how "Steve Jobs has to be rolling over in his grave given that the iPhone [insert whatever model it is now] is the size of a television." If he, (the Brit, not Steve Jobs) wanted to, "Carry that much hardware" he'd "use his iPad for his phone." A few weeks ago when his teeny tiny, pager sized phone broke (not broke as much as shattered into pieces when he dropped it accidentally) the man ran actually around town for three days with his full size (not a mini) iPad using it as a phone. He thought it was hilarious to stand in front of someone, dial them on the iPad and then hold it up to his ear and talk. He really enjoyed doing this in the car where others could see him while I drove, helpless to get away from the insanity.

Like me, Sophia knew a thing or two about suffering the whims of crazy loved ones. In the episode, *Two Rode Together* Dorothy is unnerved by the number of Sophia's friends who had seemed to die in a very short amount of time. Sophia herself is also taken off guard by the number of loved ones passing, but she perhaps chooses to not obsess over it in the same vein as Dorothy.

After relaying her fears to Rose, Dorothy is regaled with the story of *Toonder, the Mediocre Tiger* who lived in the land of *Flafluevenhaven*. It's highly probable that Dorothy didn't listen with rapt attention, or even at all. Somehow, she did get the gist which was that it is important to spend quality time with loved ones. Therefore, she lied to Sophia about a weekend at Disney World and whisked her mother away for a weekend of bonding.

Unfortunately, what amounts to sharing "quality" time for Dorothy equates to being held hostage for Sophia. Dorothy insists on looking at old home movies and photographs and discussing the past so that through that weekend she and her mother can relive fond memories and feel closer. Sophia just wants to ride Splash Mountain. When she gets a moment to hightail it out of Dorothy's sight Sophia makes her getaway with the amusement park as her goal. She winds up thwarted in her endeavor by the weather and instead retreats to the hotel bar where she is later confronted by Dorothy about her trying to escape.

Dorothy takes the opportunity to tell her mother of her fear of Sophia's mortality and her want to create quality time. Sophia wisely explains that it's not the amount of time that we spend with each other or the rehashing of our pasts that make our time together "quality." Rather, it's those little moments we steal here and there in our shared experiences. Sophia wasn't going to remember all of those past moments that Dorothy brought up that weekend, however, she was going to remember being held hostage in a hotel room in Orlando with Splash Mountain just out of reach.

In the same vein, I'm probably not going to remember years from now the actual sensation of helplessness that I've felt since my father's death. I will, however, remember bonding with my sister over our shared loss. She's most likely going to remember my plan to go to South America to get eaten by Zika infected mosquitos so I can then return home, exhume our father, inject him with said Zika and retroactively fight the brain tumors. There may have also been something in there as well about using a car battery to bring him back to life, but she informed me that if I didn't shut the idea down she was telling Mom. Deep sigh.

11

AMERICAN HORROR STORY

"No one in my family has ever seen a psychiatrist; except of course, when they were institutionalized." - Blanche

*D*uring the weeks leading up to my sister delivering my twin nieces I volunteered to watch her oldest child, my two year old niece, Vi. The Brit thought I had lost my mind, but I assured him we (yeah, he was roped into it) could handle it - she's two. What could she possibly do that would be so hard to manage?

I was so young and innocent then.

Now, in the aftermath, I have no idea how parents have managed to handle toddlers for tens of thousands of years without admitting themselves to mental institutions. I cannot fathom how they navigate the nuance of dealing with these mini-fascists. Seriously, I am genuinely surprised that we don't have entire housing complexes for the mentally unstable that are completely inhabited solely by all the poor jerks who tried to reason with a two year old.

Don't get me wrong, my niece is a wonderful person. She is beautiful, smart, and very funny. She is also quite possibly a psychopath. I honestly do not know how the human race has survived as long as it has given that babies are born helpless and two years later are certifiably insane.

I always thought toddlers were these wide eyed, adorable, short humans for whom the world was their oyster and everything was new and wonderful. Yeah, they're all that, plus they are all wild, nonsensical, chattering, crazies whose sole motivation is to break you into a snot filled, sobbing wreck incapable of loving again.

One minute my niece is the most endearing thing on the planet and in the blink of an eye she is a rage monster straight from the pits of hell. And she knows, as she stands there, looking at you, that you suspect nothing, that you're too dumb to know what is coming. Then, she smiles that super darling smile - you know, the kind of smile that makes your heart happy... when out of nowhere... KABLAM! She goes from angel to leader of the demon legions.

In less than a second the small child has gone from all smiles to machine gun subs and for no known reason. They make those loud, terrifying cries that imply to the neighbors that you have taken a child's teddy bear and cruelly ripped it apart while you make them watch and eat peas. And, the little brutes know that you're going to panic and try to figure out what could have possibly happened in that short time that it took you to blink that made them bawl and wail. Oh yes, toddlers are the brilliant lunatics of humanity and for centuries they have fooled us all!

Looking back, I'm not sure how I came to volunteer for this suicide mission. I think it was because my poor sister was SO pregnant that each time I looked in her general direction I felt so bad for her general state of misery that I needed to do something helpful. How naive I was!

When I spoke with her via FaceTime while she was in the hospital and having just delivered the twins I kept wondering how it was that fresh from a C-section she managed to look so refreshed... and young... and rejuvenated. She had just added two babies to this world. They were in the room with her! How, HOW, did she look so good? It was because she was toddler free. As long as she was in the hospital, she was safe from the terror of her home

e. The joke is on her though, in a very short amount of time she'll have not one more, but two more toddler fiends, muhahahaha-hahahaha!

After the aforementioned bonding time with my niece, the Brit and I returned home and I did what I always do in times of crisis, I looked to the Golden Girl's for wisdom. Turns out they had nothing on the topic of raising berserk toddlers. They did, however, try to rear a boxer once so I rolled with that figuring it had to be nearly the same.

In the episode, *Fiddler on the Ropes,* Sophia is sent to the bank for a $3,000 CD and instead comes home with Kid Pepe, the Cuban prizefighter. Per Dorothy's observation, it could have been worse, Sophia could have come back with magic beans.

As it turns out, caring for a Cuban boxer is in fact not all that different from caring for a two year old. Pepe didn't speak the same language as the ladies, he only wanted to fight, and he disappeared each time they took their eyes off him for a second. The difference, however, was that Pepe was running off to take violin lessons in hopes of attending Juilliard not disappearing to break, vandalize, or mutilate something. Vi doesn't bothering with the disappearing act, she blatantly makes a run for it because she knows I'm too slow and lumbering to catch her. I'm like a walrus trying to catch a cheetah only I think a walrus is faster than I am.

With Pepe, as with so many things, the girls had it all wrong. He didn't have the ambition to be a serious fighter, he was doing it for the money so as to put himself through school. He also spoke fluent English and could eloquently quote Shakespeare.

The ladies attempted to shame him for not being honest with them about himself from the get-go, but as Pepe pointed out, they didn't ask him anything about who he was, they assumed he was a brainless pugilist and really only cared for their investment in his fight. Had they taken the time to get to know him they would have discovered the many layers that made Pepe who he was. In fact, Pepe was so layered he would return in later episodes but not as

Pepe, but as (please read with an air of aplomb and a slight accent) ENRIQUE MAS! Ace consumer reporter and Rose's future boss.

After learning of Pepe's ambitions the ladies humanity kicked in and they were determined that he should take a dive in the fight. If he lost he still won enough prize money to help pay for his schooling as well as a return on the original investment that Sophia was supposed to take to the bank for her roommates. It was important to them that Pepe save his hands for the violin and for his future so they try to persuade him to take a dive. Unfortunately, his opponent got him all riled up and instead of taking the dive Pepe took a hit to the head and was knocked out. In his meeting with Juilliard he failed to remember that he was a violinist and nearly lost out on fulfilling his dreams. Luckily, Dorothy, ever quick on her feet, covertly prompted him to recite his favorite soliloquy from *Merchant of Venice* and he was instead accepted into Juilliard's Acting School.

Pepe's story lends me hope for the future of our toddlers. Perhaps they're so terrorizing and seemingly brutes because we just don't speak the same language and haven't really taken the time to know one another as people. To be fair, it is so difficult. Their interests are just so disparate from ours. They're not interested in the same music or books and they binge completely different programming. Or perhaps they really are little heathens that will grow out of their maniacal ways at least for a few years. Of course after that they tend to manifest into something much worse - teenagers. I think I just got a chill and a case of the heebie jeebies.

12

HELL'S KITCHEN

Rose: Dorothy, if the Egyptians can build the pyramids, we can move this toilet.

Dorothy: Fine. Get me twenty thousand Hebrews and I'll have it out of here in no time.

I might have mentioned in a previous chapter (or two, or ten) that I used to smoke and I loved everything about it. I loved the feel of a cigarette between my yellowed and grubby little fingers. I loved the gasp for air as the smoke hit my lungs, and I loved the inability to breathe most nights when I laid down to go to sleep (maybe I didn't love that part). The more I smokes I could get my hands on, the better off I was. This was particularly true after the divorce from my first husband.

In the first year of my life, post-marriage, I think I gazed off into the distance a lot while mindlessly chain smoking and watching traffic go by. I lived on one of the busiest streets in town and I would sit on the front porch drinking copious amounts of coffee and puffing away.

If I sat on that porch long enough everyone I knew would ha...
driven by, many of whom stopped in to see how I was doing. I'm
guessing their general take away was that I was not doing great.

Divorce is hard! She types in with all the whining intent that
sentence seems to convey. This person who had once signed on to
spend forever with me had decided that he had changed his mind.
What made it worse, was that unlike Dorothy's crap weasel ex, Stan,
mine didn't leave me for a younger, hotter model. He left me for a
crass, older woman, who, and I think I'm being fair here, was
nowhere near as cute as me. That was super devastating.

What was it about me that was no longer lovable? What did she
have that I didn't? Was it a phase? A fling? I had always thought I
was so tough and capable of handling dramatic life events. Turns
out, not so much.

I was a marshmallow and the only things holding me together
were caffeine, nicotine, and a scruffy black rabbit that had shown up
in my yard the day after the husband vacated. To this day I have no
idea from where that bunny came. And he was bedraggled to say
the least. There was roadkill out there in better shape than that
rabbit. I think his fur was being held on by duct tape. Yet, there he
was, sitting in my yard by the redwood tree as I sat on the porch,
and we just stared at one another for hours as I drank coffee and
smoked. Talk about surreal.

Looking back at it with twenty years of hindsight on my side, I
reflect and wonder how I was that person. What the heck was
wrong with me? Where did that rabbit go? Was he a super strange
figment of my imagination? Maybe something all the nicotine
coursing through my veins had conjured? Can I somehow invent
non-deadly cigarettes that still have all the nicotine?

After I started working for Child Protective Services the smoking
increased ten fold. The nice thing was that my motto at the time was
"Smoke More, Eat Less" so I was at least thin(nish). I was gray
skinned, my hair was thin, I smelled (as my mother said) like a
"smoke factory" but damn it, I was thin. The lung abuse continued
for years until I met The Brit. He too smoked, but he smoked these

he cigarettes that he made himself called "rollies." The English, even their tobacco is fancy.

When he packed his stuff to move to the States, the Brit forgot about his habit and did not bring enough materials to make rollies here in the states, and the particular tobacco he smoked and papers he used were not available in California. Thus, he quit more of out lack of equipment then any real desire to actually be done smoking. Once he had done so though, he was a nightmare to live with while I was still a smoker.

It wasn't that he harassed me about my health or even that he lectured me that made him so unbearable. It was that because he didn't smoke anymore he didn't want to go outside with me as I did. It was, and I'm quoting him here, "A ball-ache." Of course on the flip side, if I paused the t.v. to go outside alone that was also a "ball-ache" because he had to wait for me. So, he annoyed me into quitting.

I'm thankful everyday that he did, however, quitting was the worst, most painful thing I have ever done to myself and it is truly a miracle that nobody was murdered - most of all, me.

Honestly though, it was for the best. I was so committed to the art of smoking that a few weeks prior to quitting I had been in a company car at two in the morning on my way to a drug bust when I decided, "Screw it. I'm smoking in the car." There was, of course, a strict no smoking the company vehicles policy, but I was convinced everything would be fine.

I rolled the windows down on all sides, casually lit up, and then was hit by a gust of wind that blew the cherry of the cigarette up over my head and between my back and the seat. It burnt a hole in my shirt and the seat of the car.

Being the decent person I was, I returned the car, said nary a word to anybody and waited a few days for my coworker who was also a smoker, (and also kind of known for being a haphazard rule breaking chain smoker at best) to take the fall. She kept adamantly declaring that she had not smoked in the van, but nobody was having any part of her lies, including me. It was at least a decade before I confessed.

My coworker, the scapegoat, she passed away a few years ago from cancer. I'm pretty sure she's waiting for me to get there so she can finally slap me.

Many who have not religiously watched the Golden Girls may not know that both Dorothy and Rose had addiction issues of their own. Dorothy in fact had two prior struggles: gambling and smoking.

In the episode *All Bets are Off* Dorothy agrees, albeit reluctantly, to take Rose to the racetrack so that she (Rose) can work on a painting of a horse. Upon their return home from the track we find out from Sophia that fifteen years prior Dorothy was a degenerate gambler with a penchant for the ponies.

Dorothy assures her mother that she's fine and will not fall off the wagon, but of course she does. Through the rest of the episode she devolves until she is broke, out of a job, and lying to everyone around her. Then, she hits Rose up for money and what comes out of it is one of my all time favorite exchanges between the two friends:

Dorothy: Rose, I need [to borrow] money. You're just going to have to trust me.

Rose: Well, of course I trust you. You're my best friend. You can take everything I have.

Dorothy: Well, don't give me everything you have. I mean, all I need is a couple hundred bucks, you know, so that I can…

Rose: Oh, you don't owe me an explanation. Here, I want you to take my bank card, and take as much money as you need, and pay me back whenever you can.

Dorothy: Oh, thanks a lot. And don't worry. I'll have this money back before you know it.

Rose: No hurry. I trust you completely.

Dorothy: Well, Rose I mean, you shouldn't trust anyone completely.

Rose: Dorothy, if I can't trust you, whom can I trust? You're practically a sister to me.

Dorothy: Well sisters often lie, Rose. And even best friends take advantage of each other occasionally.

Rose: I don't think so.

Dorothy: Rose, you're being very naive.

Rose: I'm not naive.

Dorothy: Yes, you are. You are being naive now. Don't you see? I'm stealing your money.

Rose: I know Dorothy. But I was hoping you'd have a hard time taking advantage of someone who cares about you as much as I do.

I find it touching that while Rose is often taken for the fool, the one time she is definitely not is when her friend most wants her to be. Dorothy's guilt and shame is palpable and the scene illustrates what fine actresses Bea Arthur and Betty White were (Betty still is).

In the season before *All Bets Are Off* Rose is the roommate with the addiction in the episode *High Anxiety*. In this instance, the monkey on Rose's back is painkillers.

High Anxiety is one of those far reaching Golden Girls episodes that continues to resonate today. Thirty years after it aired hundreds of thousands of Americans continue to struggle with addictio including the present opioid crisis. I'm not sure that there isn't any family in our country who hasn't either been personally touched by the crisis or at the very least know someone who has.

Rose, like many, had been prescribed the pills by a doctor she trusted after a back injury. For over thirty years her prescription was repeatedly renewed without anyone, including Rose, questioning why she is still taking painkillers three decades after the injury.

Rose's friends have no idea about her dependence, until one day, she runs out of the pills and threatens to punch a director, who is trying to film commercial featuring Dorothy and Sophia in Blanche's kitchen.

Throughout the next few days the friends learn that Rose has a very real problem. She is at once her friendly self and a moment later a wretch who will kill for her meds. She proclaims she does not need the pills and then makes every excuse why she does. She denies that she needs help and refuses to seek treatment. The she believes that she can quit cold turkey with the support of her friends.

Blanche and Dorothy agree to help Rose and they spend an entire night in the kitchen helping her to resist the urge to give into temptation. They are quick to learn, however, that one night of success does not equate to being in recovery. Thankfully, by this point Rose is able to acknowledge that her dependence is so much bigger than she and her friends and she checks herself into a rehab program. She returns home a month later on the road to recovery and thankful for having the support system at home that she needs.

When I gave up smoking I too had a tremendous support system. All of my poor coworkers were privy to my repetitive nail polishing (every time I wanted to smoke I painted my nails, then stripped them and started over) and my horrendous mood swings. Only one took offense. Ironically, she was also a smoker.

About a month after I quit my sister did everyone a favor and took me on a two week road trip to Chicago by way of Mt. Rushore. It was deemed by our friend *The Sisters With No Misters* tour and it was just what I needed. My sister, however, is still probably ruing the day she got the idea to put Jekyll and Hyde in a Camry and tour the US. Its possible she still has night-terrors from the Ramada in Minnesota, but that's another story.

13

JUST SHOOT ME

"You'll have to excuse my mother. She survived a slight stroke which left her, if I can be frank, a complete burden." - Dorothy

*L*ately there has been a fierce debate going on in my home. The Brit tells me he's going to, "Get a shooter," and I tell him, "Hahahahahahaha. No."

It's not that I'm afraid of guns or that I don't believe people should own guns; I just happen to have more faith in the fallibility of man then I do in the safety of firearms. Now that I have three little nieces, I care more about their potential protection than I do in the Brit's right to bear arms. He's also not allowed a motorcycle, but that has more to do with my want of his being alive than it does my willingness to let him be happy. I'd rather he be alive and miserable for want of a bike then dead. I'm selfish that way. To be fair, the only driver worse than him is me, so the idea of either of us on motorcycle is scary to say the least.

My father had a few guns while I was growing up. I was nearly twenty years old before I knew this and I was thirty before I knew where he had kept them all those years. Now that's the way to do it.

he Brit speaks of the day when he'll be able to go hunting and kill things, like wabbits. I'd bet thousands of dollars that the second a bunny looked him in the eye he'd be packing up and going home, live bunny in tow. There is also a high probability of his having an accident and injuring himself or someone else, but probably not said bunny.

What is it about us humans that makes us believe that we're smart? Is it the awards and accolades we give each other for special achievements? Is it our progression as a species and our "advances" in technology, medicine, or what-have-you?

I'm not quite sure I understand our want to pat ourselves on the back for everything awesome we do when for action there is that whole pesky equal and opposite reaction thing. The atomic bomb gave us the end of the war in the Pacific in World War II... as well as the deaths of tens of thousands. The automobile gave us mobility and freedom as well as black air, black lung, and death or maiming by car accident. The printing press gave us the ability to print things en masse which also gave jerks like me the ability to publish whatever pops into our heads. See? Action leads to reaction.

For excellent examples of man's frailty and stupidity we have only to look to the GG's. They illustrated for us time and again how even the smartest of us can be so dumb. Take Dorothy: she was a very clever woman with plenty of self-accolades to go around. She also carried on a relationship with a married man not once, but twice.

The man in question was Jerry Orbach, although, later, when Dorothy meets him again he's Alex Rocco. Alex Rocco was Moe Green in the *Godfather* and poor Moe was gunned down in Vegas. If you don't know who Moe Green is, leave now to go rent the *Godfather*. We'll wait.

I lied - we're not waiting. The man that Jerry and Alex played was one Glen O'Brien. He was a teacher at a school where Dorothy had been subbing. Glen takes Dorothy on a wild, torrid, three week binge of romance and sexcapades that leaves her head over heels in love. Unfortunately for her, it's not until after said sexcapades that Glen finally tells her he's married.

Glen quantifies to Dorothy that his marriage is a "bad" one and has been for sometime. He tells her that would have left but for the kids who are by the way, over thirty years old.

At first, Dorothy takes the high road and leaves Glen. About a week later, however, she changes her mind and agrees to see him again to talk. Talking lead to a tawdry motel at the side of the highway and a renewed love affair, much to the dismay of her mother, and after a few of Sophia's well driven points, much to the dismay of Dorothy.

Like any good mom Sophia knows that her child is suffering. Dorothy, like any proud woman, denies that she's in a bad place. Sophia, however, is the wiser and advises that she knows her child spends hours at night pacing in her room because she hates herself. Again, Dorothy denies her mother is right and leaves to meet her man.

Hard headed, and stubborn, Dorothy is determined that she can be happy as Glen's mistress. That is until Glen lets it out of the bag that he doesn't plan to get divorced. His reasoning? If he did get divorced, and subsequently he and Dorothy didn't work out, he'd be alone. He would rather Dorothy be his mistress and miserable, if that meant he didn't have to possibly be alone someday. Pretty nice guy, right?

It was at this point that Dorothy found where she had been hiding her self respect and ended it for good. Well, not quite for good. Old Glen popped up again four years later (this is when he was the aforementioned Alex Rocco who was Moe Green... speaking of, did you finish that movie yet?).

In an episode of Season five aptly titled, *Cheaters*, Glen comes crawling out of the woodwork divorced and unbearably alone. Of course Sophia is still wary of him, but after he calls, Dorothy agrees to see him. Then she agrees to sleep with him. Then she agrees to let him meet her mother. Somewhere in there Glen attempts to get her to agree to marry him, because as we know, he doesn't like being alone.

Confused about the decision before her, Dorothy gets some unexpected help when Glen's wife calls while she is with him. Being the upstanding guy he is, Glen lies and says he's alone which gives Dorothy the push she needs to realize, he's still a mensch. Sophia, though she seems to get along well with Glen upon meeting him, still knows that there is still inherently something not quite right, but she lets Dorothy make the decision to marry him without her input this time. Maybe she knew Dorothy would do the right thing?

I had a similar situation with mother. It wasn't about a man though, it was about cosmetics.

It was the summer of 7th grade, and all of the other girls had secretly bought make-up to put on during the bus ride to school. Like them, I too was prohibited from wearing make-up so young. And, like them, I too bought make-up to apply while on the bus to school.

That morning my mother, the puma she is, noiselessly snuck into my room just seconds after I had snuck the contraband into my ugly, yellow, 80's felt sac of a purse.

Very sweetly she said, "I know a lot of the girls will be going to school today and putting on make-up behind their parents backs. I want you to know, it means a lot to me that you respect me enough not to do the same."

As soon as she had left the room, out came the drawer, and into it went the make-up, not to be seen again until I was sixteen and the ban lifted. Years later I asked my mother if she had seen it in my room or had she seen me putting it in my bag that day. She said she just instinctively knew that I had some and that I was going to take it to school if she didn't say something.

So, what is the moral to this story? Mother's know everything and the Brit can't have a bike or a gun, but if he wants, he can have a wabbit.

14

RULES OF ENGAGEMENT

Rose: It wasn't a rat! It was a cute little mouse!

Dorothy: Rose, it doesn't wear white gloves and work at Disneyland! We're talking about a rodent!

Over the last few years we have been told that in America we the people are increasingly at odds with one another. Pundits, journalists, bloggers, those people at parties who pretend to be in the know, our uncles at the holidays - all of them say the same thing; we Americans are in a state of constant animosity where nobody sees eye-to-eye and there has never been a more divided time in our politics. I think they negate a nasty little skirmish we fought known as the Civil War but that's just me.

The Golden Girls were also not impervious to political division and like many families they were nearly destroyed by their difference of opinion. That's right, the ladies were nearly brought down by their political interests or more accurately, a politicians' want of someone, anyone, to interested in his campaign.

The episode *Strange Bedfellows*, sees Dorothy, Blanche, and Rose supporting their chosen candidate for some office one Gil Kessler.

Gil is so nice and his life so scandal free that he isn't just a safe a choice for a political seat, he's as Sophia refers to him, "bland as mayonnaise." Yet, the roommates throw their collective weight behind his campaign and even throw him a campaign party in their home. This is where things get a little dicey; not for Gil, but for the roommates.

After the soiree, Blanche realizes that Gil left behind a folder of paperwork and she decides to be kind and return it to him at his home. Unfortunately for Blanche she is photographed entering Gil's home, and as later pointed out by the newspapers his wife is conveniently out of town. The next day, a political scandal had Miamians far and wide wanting to know who the mystery woman visiting Kessler could be.

Upon seeing the photograph in the paper, Rose and Dorothy recognize the clothes, build, and hair in the photo and immediately believe that Blanche has slept with Gil. Blanche proclaims her innocence, yet her friends refuse the idea that a leopard can change her spots and Blanche's proclamations fall on deaf ears. It's the one time Blanche finds herself in a pickle for *not* sleeping with someone.

To me, this episode goes a long way in showing us how easy it is to buy into what is easy rather than to put in the work to believe in something new or different. Is this due to inherent laziness? Or, is there something biological that makes humans incapable of hearing (or seeing) something new and embracing it?

I struggle with this inability to grow beyond my beliefs all the time - even when they're challenged by people whom I respect, and sometimes even with irrefutable evidence biting me in the behind. A good example of this is my once blinding, unwavering devotion to Ronald Reagan.

Yep, the Gipper and I go way back to when I was a little kid at the age when I knew everything my parents said was true, gospel even. There was no man, woman, or other fourth grader alive capable of dissuading me that my folks could be wrong about anything. Hence, when another kid dared to dream that someone other than Ronald Reagan was going to win the 1984 election I had straight from my dad's mouth this was not the case and I willing to fight for something I had no idea about.

Side note: I am not as one might expect based on my Reagan love, a dyed in the wool Republican. I'm a registered Independent who has voted on both sides of the aisle (I like to keep my options open). I was, however, raised by a dyed in the wool Republican.

My dad was so Republican (sounds like the start of a bad joke) he was the only person I had ever known who hadn't a clue where he was the day Kennedy was shot. My mom - she could tell you what she was wearing at that exact moment in time she heard that terrible news it's so etched in her memory. Not my father. He wasn't going to get bogged down in the details of anything involving a Democrat, not even when those details applied to himself.

My father was so Republican, that when he found out that I, his eldest (and I'd like to believe favorite and most beloved child), had registered as an American Independent you could tell something inside him had broken.

We were having one of those super fun family dinners not long after I turned eighteen where my sister and I took turns digging at one another by angrily telling the Units something horrendous the other one had done. My poor mother watched us go back and forth, turning her head from side to side with increasing horror as sentences like this were blurted out:

Me: "Oh yeah, well Kim stole a car and went joyriding! (She was all of fourteen at the time)."

Kim: "Tiffany smokes!" Cue deep gasp from my mother.

Me: "Kimberley has a bottle of Sangria - in her closet!" Choking sound from my mother's end of the table.

Kim: "Tiffany registered as an Independent!"

Everyone could hear my father's fork falling through the empty space between him and the table and we watched disgust flood his face in slo-mo. All the while the word "noooooooooooooo......." was coming out of his mouth with equal protractedness. Following the cacophony of ringing made by the fork hitting his plate before plummeting to the floor below, Dad took a deep breath, turned his head to me and said, "I can't believe a daughter of mine could.... You might as well throw away your vote. I raised you better than that." Then, with great dignity, he got up from the table and strode proudly to the living room to seek comfort in his barcalounger.

My mother shook her head and then naturally had to ground us for all the other things that had come out. I think it was two to three weeks later before my father could look me in the eye again and after that, it was never the same. The level of betrayal that I had committed toward him by my sinister act of making my own political decisions had nearly killed the guy. But back to the Gipper....

I remember the playground in fourth grade where Crystal Whats-her-face and I were discussing politics over what would become a very heated game of Skill. If you don't know or haven't heard of Skill it's a very intricate, chess like game, where one person bounces a ball over a line (real or imaginary will do) to another person who then, wait for it, bounces it back. It was previewed as an Olympic sport at the aught eight games but was deemed too difficult for audiences to follow.

So, there we were, playing Skill when the aforementioned heated political discussion came about. I don't know who instigated it. It was probably her. I'm not even sure why someone had instigated it as we were seriously, like eight or nine years old... maybe ten? We were whatever age fourth graders are. Alas! The 1984 election was obviously weighing very heavy on our minds thus the topic was introduced by Crystal Something-or-other who told me with confidence that her daddy said Walter Mondale was going to win.

I of course, had it on my father's good authority and impeccable record of voting for Republicans that Reagan was going to be walking away with it in a landslide. Things were said that I can never take back, as well as other things I'll take with me to my grave (mostly because I can't remember at all what was actually said). Then as it so often happens in fourth grade playground fights about political candidates, Crystal Watch-ma-jigger hit the ball to me way too hard.

Affronted, and well within my rights, I threw it at her head. She dramatically gasped and accused me of trying to maim her ugly mug. Out of nowhere, she strode up and punched me in the side while attempting a head lock of sorts (I'm pretty certain she was like five feet shorter than me and I was only like four foot something to begin with, hence I have no idea how this came about). So, I did the only thing I could do. I bit her arm. It was a going-for-broke, my rep is riding on this kind of bite too. There were teeth marks and everything. If Crystal Who-actually-knows-or-cares hadn't been a vampire blood would have been drawn.

Naturally, I was in a crazy amount of trouble with my Units over this, although, I'd like to think my father was secretly super proud. I tried to explain, it was the other kid's fault - she was talking nonsense and spewing lies. My mother wasn't budging though. I probably got detention for it at school and there is a very high probability that I was grounded or spanked or both, but damn it - if I had to - I'd totally go back and do it again. Mostly because I don't have extremely fond memories of Crystal Whiny-britches and I'd like another go at her. There was a moral to this story…. Reagan… Blanche… right!

Poor Blanche, she was victim to her own patterns and previous choices. Because she was usually a wanton slut her friends believed this to be true even when she protested her innocence. Gil didn't help matters either, he held a press conference where he told Miami that Blanche was indeed the floozy who had been photographed coming out of his house following a torrid night of sex and debauchery.

Rose and Dorothy took his word over that of their friend which could be why it hurt Blanche so much to be disbelieved. That, and her pals actively shunned her for days. It wasn't until Blanche was able to get Gil to do the right thing and hold a new press conference explaining he did not have an affair that her friends came around and realized their mistake.

My mistake, was having been wholeheartedly convinced in the awesomeness of Ronald Reagan. When it came out not too long ago that he, like many others before him was caught left handed being a racist I didn't want to believe it. Not my Ronnie! Tapes were released of him saying terrible things about Africans to Nixon. Even in light of the tapes I kept denying that it could be him. I had gone to the mat for that man!

I waited for several days for a new revelation to come to light; something, anything, that would exonerate him. Nothing. It was him, and deep down, I knew it to be true, I had heard the tapes and I knew that voice anywhere.

I had banked my precious elementary school reputation on a candidate that in the end, disappointed me. Where Blanche could for once keep it in her pants, the guy who we thought was but one of a handful of Commanders-in-Chief who at the very least hadn't been a bigot actually was. Sometimes it works like that. The people we admire turn out to be something we really didn't want them to be. If you're wondering what happened to Gil, it turned out that he was still bland as well as a liar. Oh, and he used to be a woman before his operation.

I like to believe that my father was happy to know that he was raising a daughter who so hero worshipped him that she would engage in fisticuffs to defend his beliefs. That is of course until I betrayed him by becoming an Independent. If that wasn't betrayal enough for dad, four years after the initial dining table incident there was a new revelation to come to light. Kim and Tiffany were once again debasing each other in a rousing round of, "Oh yeah! Well, your other daughter...." when things got heated:

Me: "Oh yeah, well Kim ditched school for an entire day"

Kim: "Tiffany killed a priest!" Cue deep gasp from my mother.

Me: "Kimberley registered as an Independent!" I can still hear that fork falling…

15

ONE DAY AT A TIME

Rose: [about Stan's latest invention] What's a "Zborny"?

Dorothy: I put up with it for thirty-eight years, Rose. Trust me, you don't want to know.

I think it's easy for those of us living in 2019 to feel that the struggle for women's rights and equality has seen some pretty awesome progression as of late. The #metoo movement has been a huge victory in the fight against the traditional zeitgeist and our traditionally male dominated society has finally allowed for many of those with real power to see consequences for preying upon others.

Perhaps in some cases, those consequences haven't been as entirely satisfying as we may want, but there's always hope they'll bring back tarring and feathering people.

What we might forget, or not even know about, is the efforts that were being made in the past by (among many, many others), the Golden Girls. In multiple episodes the ladies take on a number of women's issues including: discrimination against women, age discrimination, domestic violence, unwanted pregnancy, societal rejection, and even, sexual harassment.

By the end of the first season of the show we, the audience, are well aware of Blanche's sexual prowess. She is the type of character who is extremely vocal about sex and her ensuing escapades. She makes no bones (pun intended) about who she is, even joking that she couldn't wear virginal white to her wedding because not even she would have been able to keep a straight face. This is exactly why she is the perfect example of how sexual harassment can effect everyone, including those who are confident, strong women.

Having returned to school in an effort to get a promotion, Blanche finds that she is failing her Psychology class. Rose and Dorothy encouraged her to study harder and to talk to the teacher, Mr. Cooper, about her inability to grasp the classwork. Mr. Cooper as it turns out is a schmuck who offers Blanche the opportunity to pass his class by doing some "extra credit." Wink, wink, nudge, nudge. Uncertain what to say or do, Blanche returns home to again seek the counsel of her roommates.

Blanche admits to them that she often uses her body to get what she wants out of men rather than using her wits and intellect. Rose advises that maybe it's time for her to start using that intellect, and Dorothy concurs. They offer to help her study so that she can ace the final exam and pass the class. More importantly, however, they also convince her to take the step that many of us are afraid to do — report the harassment.

Blanche subsequently meets with the school dean who advises her that without corroboration from a witness there was nothing that he could do to help her. She had been defeated by a broken system. A system that has inherently favored men and taught women that their voice is not equal to that of their male counterparts.

A perfect example of this is in the two part episode, *Sick and Tired*. Dorothy has been suffering for months from exhaustion and an overwhelming feeling of being run down and not all together well. She seeks help from a number of physicians including a very young and yet still very bald Jeffrey Tambor (who was himself reported for harassment years later on the set of *Transparent*).

One after another, the doctors, and Jeffrey Tambor, tell Dorothy they can't find anything wrong with her. Tambor goes so far as to tell her that her problem is probably mental and implies that she's just a hysterical woman with no real health issues. Fortunately for Dorothy, Richard Mulligan is playing Harry Weston, their neighbor who is a pediatrician.

Harry helps Dorothy get to a specialist where it is discovered that she suffers from Chronic Fatigue Syndrome - an illness that many today still do not believe is a real medical diagnosis. I'm chronically fatigued, but I'm pretty certain mine has more to do with staying up till 3am playing Disney's Emoji Blitz on my phone than anything else.

I am hopeful, as I'm sure many are that the #metoo movement is just the start of real change. I do however, worry sometimes that the ideations about women are too ingrained in our societal norms.

My sister had just had first daughter, Vi, when the movie *Wonder Woman* was released. We went to see it with our spouses and like many women we both had that moment of swelling pride that the female superhero on the screen wasn't the sidekick or the crazy villain, but rather SHE, this truly awesome person, was the star of the movie and all on her own was capable of saving the day.

Afterwards, we women beamed with delight, there was finally a superhero portrayed on the big screen that also had a vagina and she was magnificent. Of course our husbands didn't get it and started rattling on about other "awesome female characters" like Ripley from *Alien* and Sarah Conner from *Terminator*.

We tried to explain to them that yes, Ripley, Sarah Conner, and other badass women were badass, but that wasn't the point. Most little girls (most, not all) do not grow up idolizing the women like Ripley and Sarah Conner because they are from rated "R" movies. We didn't grow up wanting to be Sarah and Ripley because we didn't get to see Sarah and Ripley! Wonder Woman on the other hand, is rated "PG-13" which equates to many tween and teens getting to see this amazing women in years crucial to the formation of our identities.

In the case of Wonder Woman I would honestly let my nieces see it as soon as they interested in doing so. Girls need role models who are strong, kind, and most importantly discerning of that which is right or wrong.

So, our point to the Brit and the bro-in-law was that up until Wonder Woman's movie men had dominated the superheroes we saw in the theater. Until 2017 we had had a few Supermen, multiple Batman's, an Ironman, Ant-Man, Deadpool, Captain America, Black Panther, even several Spider-Men. But Wonder Woman - she was a first and she belonged to us women. She was ours and she was no quivering mewl.

Wonder Woman represents all that is awesome about being female and she is glorious. The men folk argued there had been a Wonder Woman t.v. show - again, not the point. They argued Wonder Woman was in the horrible Batman and Superman movie. Again, this was not the point. They didn't get it, but it didn't really matter if they did, for in 2019 someone even bigger and badder came to the big screen - *Captain Marvel*.

I don't know what my brother-in-law thought of *Captain Marvel*, but the Brit finally understood what we women had been talking about. Carol Danvers, aka Captain Marvel, wasn't just a hero. She was a one-of-a-kind, spaceship busting, Flerken handling, "I am going to save the day and Marvel can't defeat Thanos without my power" kind of hero. It was the first time that the fate of not just mankind, but of the entire Marvel Movie universe depended on a woman to rescue them from decimation.

I have to note that had Marvel given the Scarlet Witch the screen time that character deserved she and Captain Marvel could have destroyed Thanos without any of the others. I'm digressing again.... Captain Marvel... yes!

Captain Marvel is a character which along with Wonder Woman

we can be proud to share with the little girls who are coming up behind us. What sets Carol apart is that she didn't need a man to fall in love with while saving the world. Wonder Woman had a love affair with her man pal Steve Trevor, but at the end of the day Captain Marvel sent Jude Law home in a spaceship without so much as a kiss on the cheek. It was marvelous.

16

MODERN FAMILY

Dorothy: [picks up a crab on the table] Oh, look at this one. Scrunched up little frown. Kinda reminds me of my mother.

[She picks up a crab hammer and smashes it]

*L*ast Friday my friend Hernandez and I attended the funeral of our former supervisor's husband. To clarify - Hernandez is not Hernandez's first name. It's not even her last name (anymore). Sixteen years ago, when I first met her, and right before she became my sister from another mister (I might be too old and way too white to get away with that, but I'm gonna try) we were working in the same office. Her first name is Marie and my boss at the time was also a Marie. So, I just called them each by their last name to save time. It doesn't save me time now as I often have to explain why poor Hernandez is Hernandez and not Marie (her first name) and then I have to explain her last name isn't Hernandez, and then I usually get some kind of sass from whomever I'm speaking with for not calling Hernandez Marie. At this point, however, she's been Hernandez for so long she's taking that moniker to the grave.

If ever she gets divorced and goes back to Hernandez I'll already be prepared. I'm a good friend. Thoughtful even.

So, there we were, H and I (oh, I call her H to save time because Hernandez just takes forever to say) at the funeral of our former supervisor's husband. The supervisor in question is not the 2nd Marie, but rather Karen. Karen's family, like mine, has unfortunately been having one craptastic of a 2019.

Back in December, 2018, after my father had been diagnosed, he did two stints in the local hospital. One the week of the diagnosis, and one that started December 27th after he took a nasty spill at home. While we were there with dad my mom, sister, and I wandered into the cafeteria and were eating when a very familiar face appeared, it was Karen. I think we were both surprised to see one another there in that godforsaken place. Each of us started speaking at once and it came to light that her husband also had a brain tumor. He was ten years younger than my dad and like my folks, they had been together for nearly fifty years. I felt so sad for her.

Over the course of the ensuing weeks my dad seemed to be getting better, but the news for her family seemed to be getting worse. The prognosis was grim, but the doctors were going to try to help him. Then, my dad suddenly slipped away and immediately I felt like the only person on this planet who understood how (outside of my mom and sister of course) it hurt was Karen. On the day of the funeral she messaged me to advise that had she not had to be at home to take care of her sick husband she would have been there with me at the church. To this day that was an incredibly touching moment for in my life. This person whose own life was hell took time out of her pain to reach out to me in mine.

My relationship with Karen has now morphed into something beyond what it was. We went to lunch several months back (post my father's death, pre-her husband's) and with one another, we were able to talk about the new shape that our families had taken because of cancer. She asked questions about what it is like going forward once her husband leaves her. I asked about her husband's treatments, the doctor's, his reactions, the nurses. She needed to know what to expect when he was gone. I needed to know there wasn't anything different we could have done that would have saved my father. We each knew that the other wasn't going say something that magically made everything better, but there was a comfort in sharing with someone we loved the understanding that it seriously sucked.

These bonds that we make - the connections we forge with other people, whether they be family, spouses, friends, or even pets; these are so truthfully the ties that bind us. Our connections to others keep us whole. They sustain us when all is bleak, they cheer our shattered hearts, and they create the memories upon which we draw when we need levity to break the spell of melancholy that can invade our lives. The next to last episode of the *Golden Girls* is a great reminder of this, for in that episode the true relationship of the ladies is tested when Rose suffers a heart attack and must undergo triple bypass surgery.

While waiting in the hospital for news of their friend, Dorothy, Sophia, and Blanche are attempting to keep each other's spirits up by sharing their favorite stories about Rose. Kirsten, Roses' daughter catches the women in a moment she perceives as levity at a time that she believes should be honored with reflection and worry. Due to this misinterpretation of the roommates true feelings and intent, Kirsten unilaterally makes a decision that upon her mother's release, Rose is coming home to Minnesota. Because she's Rose's biological family she has this right. A right that Dorothy, Blanche, and Sophia do not because they are not Rose's "family."

As words go, "Family" is one that is defined by so many different things. It encompasses not just the blood relatives we love, but also those with whom we have chosen to spend our time and to share our love. Kirsten failed to take into account that her mother's roomies were her family. They loved her as much as anybody else did. It's not until she sees Dorothy, Blanche, and Sophia's concerns for Rose, coupled with Rose's own defiance about returning to

Minnesota, that Kirsten realizes that she had jumped to conclusions and made a mistake regarding her mother's future.

In the final episode of the series, *One Flew Out of the Cuckoo's Nest*, Dorothy is leaving her friends to marry Blanche's uncle, Leslie Nielsen. After the ceremony, and as she's preparing to leave for her future life, Dorothy calls her mother and two best friends her angels. I think this is true of all of our friends and loved ones, they are our angels. They make us better, make us stronger, and make us believe in everything that is possible for our lives. They hold us up and implore us to do and be everything we can dream possible for ourselves. When we've lost our dreams, they help us to find new ones. They share our laughter and tears and sometimes even cheesecake...

THE FINAL FAREWELL

Dorothy: Well...

Blanche: Well...

Rose: Yea...

Sophia: ...I guess this is it.

Dorothy: *[nodding]* Right. Listen-

Blanche: Dorothy, you don't have to say anything.

Rose: What can you say about 7 years of fights and laughter, secrets, and cheesecake...

Dorothy: Just that...it's been very... it has been an experience that I'll always keep close to my heart. *[sobbing]* And that these are memories that...I'll wrap myself in when the world gets cold and I forget that there are people who are warm and loving and...

Blanche: We love you, too...*[girls embrace and cry]*...You'll always be a part of us.

Dorothy: Your friendship was something I never expected at this point of my life, and I could never asked for a better surprise

Blanche: *[sobbing]* That's how we feel too.

Dorothy: I have to go.

Rose: Dorothy......is this goodbye?

Dorothy: *[walks to the door, looks at the girls and nods]*...I love you, always *[leaves room while the girls stare at the door. Dorothy re-appears from the door]* Oh god, I love you! *[girls embrace again]*

Blanche: *[sobbing]* Oh Dorothy...Dorothy...

Dorothy: *[sobbing]* Lucas is waiting *[heads to the door again, looks at girls]* You're angels...all of you *[leaves room again while the girls stare at the door again. Dorothy comes out from the backyard hall]* OH GOD, I'LL MISS YOU!!! *[girls embrace once more]* Listen I have a flight... *[heads for the door once more]* ...**you'll always be my sisters...** *[sobbing]* **always.**